Is Suu Kyi a racist?

Shwe Lu Maung

A publication of
    Shahnawaz Khan
    USA

Printed and Published
in USA by Shahnawaz Khan.

The Covers and interiors are designed and
edited by the Khan publication team. Last
review on November 11, 2014.

Front cover depicts peoples asking a question to
Buddha.

Front cover picture:
Mahayana Dharmacakra Buddha: the picture
was taken at Sachse Buddhist Temple
by the author in 2010.

Is Suu Kyi a racist?
ISBN 13:978-1-928840-11-4
ISBN 10:1-928840-11-6

To my three wise friends

Is Suu Kyi a racist?

Table of Contents

Acknowledgment

- ❖ I am grateful to my friends who read the initial manuscript and give suggestions and correct the typos. In view of their security the names are withheld.
- ❖ My thanks are also due to the 88 generation Rakhaing students and youths, and the Rakhaing revolutionaries for providing the pictures and information on the subjects and matters of interest. On account of their security the names not mentioned.
- ❖ With due thanks, great appreciation is recorded here for the unyielding contributions of the Khan publication team.

Preface

I am a student of biological science and I became a Zoology Honours student at Rangoon University in 1963, after reading Charles Darwin's *On the Origin of Species*. I am a *Homo sapiens* and we are all *Homo sapiens,* belonging to the Family Hominidae, under the Order Primates. This is my dogma. Pretty bad, ya?

Unfortunately, among the 7.23 billion human beings the number of biologist is absolutely insignificant. The biologists are daily bullied by the non-biologists on this planet, Earth. Miserable!

There is no such a thing known as 'race' in the biological science. Nevertheless, the concept of race is the deal of the daily business in the human society. Commonly, the white, black, brown, and yellow races are the mainstay of the business across the world. In Myanmar though, there are 135 races; every shade of color, every shape of facial feature, every tone of dialect, and every rite of culture is classified into a different race. The people of next village belong to a different race and great caution is given in dealing them. They could be our enemy! Officially, there are 135 races in Myanmar. Amazing!

For example, the Rakhine and the Bama have the same alphabets, literature, language, religion, and culture. The only difference one can detect is that the Rakhine pronounce 'r' like

'Rangoon' but the Bama have no 'r' sound and they say 'Yangon'. All the way from the good old days to good new days, they agree that they are the different races and thus licensed to kill and destroy each other. The Bama is the winner. They destroyed the Rakhine kingdom in 1403 and finally in 1784; two thirds of the Rakhine population were eliminated. The Rakhine destroyed Bama Taungnu Kingdom in 1599– only once, and they could not kill all the Bama; too populous the Bama were.

The racial hierarchy in Myanmar is a form of drug-resistant malarial parasite. I call it *Plasmodium myanmaracium* in honor of the *Plasmodium falciparum* that nearly killed me twice, once in 1967 and second time in 1990. It smartly uses the mosquitoes as the vectors to bite, infect, and finally kill the host. It was not surprising that I ended up in the United States.

Today, the world views that Myanmar people are the most friendly people and the tourists flock there in spite of the mosquito bites. After all, Myanmar civilization is millennium old and her culture is exotic. There is also an Oxford-educated Lady, no less than a Nobel Laureate, with a sweet smile on her pretty face at all times.

On the other hand, the international news headlines have been flashing with the reports of racial killings and conflicts, but the Lady is silent on these issues, prompting me to quietly ask a soft question. This shall be done in my leisure time and in a most informal manner.

Is Suu Kyi a racist?

Shwe Lu Maung

Prologue

Racism is a very powerful belief and it has been practiced by every nation, and is still being practiced by some nations. Accordingly, 'racism' is a hot subject of study by numerous scholars. Some definitions of racism are given below.

Racism definition

1. **racism,** *also called racialism , any action, practice, or belief that reflects the racial worldview—the ideology that humans are divided into separate and exclusive biological entities called "races," that there is a causal link between inherited physical traits and traits of personality, intellect, morality, and other cultural behavioral features, and that some races are innately superior to others.*

Source:
http://www.britannica.com/EBchecked/topic/488187/racism

2. *A belief that race is the primary determinant of human traits and capacities and that racial differences produce an inherent superiority of a particular race.*

Source:

http://www.merriam-
    webster.com/dictionary/racism?
    show=0&t=1369149510

A distinguished professor of clinical psychology, Jefferson M. Fish, Ph.D. (http://jeffersonfish.com/) explained racism as follow.

"The word racism is now used in a variety of ways, but substituting other words for each meaning and employing it in a particular anthropological sense can clarify matters and make for greater precision--like distinguishing lasagna from spaghetti or macaroni... The German "Nuremberg Laws" (1935) established a pseudo-scientific basis for racial discrimination.

I would argue for a particular anthropological definition, even though it may seem strange on first view–racism is the belief that culture is inherited. That is, it is a belief that groups of people behave in distinctive ways not because they have learned to do so, but because their members share some inherited essence (called "blood"; or sometimes "genes"--but without reference to specific DNA sequences)."

Source:
http://www.psychologytoday.com/blog/looking-in-the-cultural-mirror/201101/how-should-racism-be-defined

Racism is a very big subject. Numerous scholars have contributed toward the better understanding and overcoming of racism. The Wikipedia article 'racism'[1] at is a good starting point for the study. "The Myth of Race" (Argo-Navis, 2012, ISBN-13: 978-0786754366) by Jefferson M. Fish, and "Encyclopedia of Race, Ethnicity and Society" (SAGE Publications, Inc, 2008, ISBN: 9781412926942) by Richard T Schaefer, Ph.D., a distinguished sociologist, http://www.schaefersociology.net/, are good books to read.

In our days we have seen severe racism in Germany (Nazism), the United States of America (Slavery and Segregation), and in South Africa (Apartheid). Today, the world is witnessing the rise of Myanmar Racism which is characterized by alienation, segregation, subordination, and negation, accompanied by destruction of the home and villages, establishment of concentration camps, planned deprivation of food and water, targeted birth control,[2] and above all organized killing.[3] I have warned the world about the Rakhaing Neo-Nazism in my book *The Price of Silence*, published in 2005.[4]

---

[1] https://en.wikipedia.org/wiki/Racism

[2] Paul Vrieze and Zarni Mann, Govt sets two-child limit for Rohingyas in Northern Arakan, The Irrawaddy, Monday, May 20, 2013. http://www.irrawaddy.org/archives/35017. Accessed on May 24, 2013.

[3] For a comprehensive report see 'All you can do is pray', Human Rights Watch, ISBN: 978-1-62313-0053., 2013. http://www.hrw.org/.

[4] Shwe Lu Maung, *The Price of Silence: Muslim-Buddhist War of Bangladesh and Myanmar – A Social Darwinist's Analysis*, DewDrop Arts & Technology,USA, 2005.

The world has responded racism with the Universal Declaration of Human Rights[5] but to no effect in real life.

Myanmar racism, which is a strong component of Myanmarism, is not new.[6] It has roots in its history. In today's Myanmar, in particular in the Rakhine State, Adolf Hitler is revered as a hero and Nazism is incorporated in the ruling party doctrine. For example, the Rakhine State government and its ruling party, Rakhine Nationalities Development Party (RNDP), treat the Rohingya in the same way the Third Reich treated the Jews. They were supported by the nationwide 969 Buddhist movement and the bodies known as the Organization for the Protection of Race and Religion, in every city and town. The Union Parliament of Myanmar, where Suu Kyi is a member lawmaker and opposition leader, not only ignores the rising racism but also denies the existence of racism in Myanmar.

Under such uneasy atmosphere that I ask the uneasy question: Is Suu Kyi a racist?
The world needs to know.

---

[5] https://www.un.org/en/documents/udhr/
[6] Shwe Lu Maung, *The Price of Silence: Muslim-Buddhist War of Bangladesh and Myanmar – A Social Darwinist's Analysis*, DewDrop Arts & Technology,USA, 2005 and Shwe Lu Maung, *The Rakhine State Violence*, Vol. I & II, Shahnawaz Khan Publication (USA), 2014.

1
Is Suu Kyi a racist?

THERE are three main reasons why the question of Suu Kyi racism arises. These are (1) the Rohingya issue, (2) the Kachin War, and (3) the Bama Supremacy.

1. The Rohingya Issue

Poor Aung San Suu Kyi! In the peak of her popularity, just after the 2nd day of May 2012 when she was sworn in as the elected Member of the Lower House of Myanmar Parliament (Pyithu Hluttaw or People's Assembly), and just before her historic European tour in June 2012, she got caught in the century-old Rakhine-Rohingya fiasco, which was a manifestation of the classic Myanmar racism as well as the classic Buddhist-Muslim war.

On her European tour, she was questioned on the burning issue of the Rohingya citizenship in Myanmar. She replied that she did not know whether they were the Myanmar nationals or the Bengali illegal immigrants.[7]

Her answer raised the eyebrow of the world to such an extent that many of her international followers and admirers started

---

[7] http://www.reuters.com/article/2012/06/18/us-suukyi-violence-idUSBRE85H1MY20120618

reviewing her status of 'democracy icon' and 'pioneer of Myanmar Human Rights'. On the other hand her Myanmar disciples are pretty happy with her stand and silence on the Rohingya issue.

Exhibit-1
Suu Kyi replied: "I don't know"
Google search result, 10/29/2012

Aung San Suu Kyi facing the challenge of a divided nation | World ...
blogs.channel4.com/world...suu-kyi...a.../22639 - United Kingdom
Jun 21, 2012 – When asked whether the Rohingya should be regarded as Burmese, she **replied, "I don't know**." Ms **Suu Kyi** added, unhelpfully, that the ...

Aung San Suu Kyi has become the subject of criticism | The Kuala ...
www.kualalumpurpost.net/aung-san-suu-kyi-has-become-the-subject...
Aug 27, 2012 – Asked whether the Rohingya should be granted Myanmar citizenship, **Suu Kyi replied** curtly: "I **don't know**." The news report from UK daily The ...

Suu Kyi's silence on Rohingya draws rare criticism
bigstory.ap.org/article/suu-kyis-silence-rohingya-draws-rare-criticism
Aug 16, 2012 – Asked if the Rohingya should be granted Myanmar citizenship, the Oxford- educated **Suu Kyi replied: "I don't know**."Canadian-based academic ...

Now, the word *Rohingya* has become a *taboo*. One can get killed for saying the word *Rohingya*. As of August 22, 2014, Matthew Russell Lee of the Inner City Press has a concise report on the issue,[8] and a video clip[9] of the UN's humanitarian deputy Kyung-wha Kang who explains why and where the United Nations use or do not use the word *Rohingya*. According to Kang, the UN officials do not use the terminology in public. In the Recent visit in

---

[8] http://www.innercitypress.com/kerry1rohingyan0081014.html
[9] https://www.youtube.com/watch?v=P7pODubGemU&feature=youtube

August 2104, the US State Secretary John Kerry also did not use the word *Rohingya*. The UN Special Rapporteur on the Situation of Human Rights in Myanmar, Yanghee Lee, explained the taboo on Rohingya as follows in her statement at the Yangon International Airport, Myanmar, 26 July 2014.[10]

"Issues around terminology and citizenship are particularly sensitive. I was repeatedly told not to use the term 'Rohingya' as this was not recognized by the Government. Yet, as a human rights independent expert, I am guided by international human rights law. In this regard, the rights of minorities to self-identify on the basis of their national, ethnic, religious and linguistic characteristics is related to the obligations of States to ensure non-discrimination against individuals and groups, which is a central principle of international human rights law. I also note that various human rights treaty bodies and intergovernmental bodies, including the Committee on the Rights of the Child, which I chaired for four years and of which I was a member for ten years, the Human Rights Council and the General Assembly use the term 'Rohingya'."

As a matter of fact, I (the author) have also been *sternly advised* not to use the word *Rohingya* if I want to stay *free of troubles*.

---

[10] http://www.ohchr.org/EN/NewsEvents/Pages/DisplayNews.aspx?NewsID=14909&LangID=E

The world has become the hostage of Myanmar racism.

Restoration and advancement of democracy in Myanmar owe a great deal to the international planetary citizens and their solidarity with the Myanmar people in their fight for democracy against the brutal military colonialism. The enshrinement of human rights is the foundation of the modern-day democracy. When Myanmar people, with racial and religious hatred, turn violent against the downtrodden Rohingya and when their democracy icon shows ignorance or negligence and remains silent on the crucial human rights issue the question arises all over the world.

2. The Kachin War

The Kachin War, today, represents Myanmar chronic internal conflict that is known as the civil war, rebellion, revolution, liberation struggle, insurgency and *et cetera*, depending on the observer's bias.[11] When we transcend the bias and reach out the plane of humanism we encounter grave concern of human rights violations, which have been recorded by various rights groups including the Amnesty International (AI), Human Rights Watch (HRW), Fortify Rights (FR), and United Nations Human Rights (UNHR). Some examples are given below.[12]

---

[11] Shwe Lu Maung, *Burma Nationalism and Ideology*, University Press Ltd., Dhaka, 1989

[12] The last access to the URL links given here was on August 18, 2014

1. *Myanmar: Protect civilians caught in the Kachin state conflict, investigate attacks*, 15 January 2013.
http://www.amnesty.org/en/news/myanmar-protect-civilians-caught-kachin-state-conflict-investigate-attacks-2013-01-15

2. *"Untold Miseries," Wartime Abuses and Forced Displacement in Burma's Kachin State.*
http://www.hrw.org/sites/default/files/reports/burma0312ForUpload_1.pdf

3. *Myanmar: End Wartime Torture in Kachin State and northern Shan State*, June 09, 2014.
http://www.fortifyrights.org/publication-20140609.html

4. *Statement of the Special Rapporteur on the Situation of Human Rights in Myanmar*, Yangon International Airport, Myanmar, 26 July 2014.
http://www.ohchr.org/EN/NewsEvents/Pages/DisplayNews.aspx?NewsID=14909&LangID=E

In Myanmar vocabulary there is only one word that covers nation, race, tribe, ethnicity, or clan. The word is *lumyo*, which literally means the kind of human. For example Bama lumyo means the Bama kind of human, Kachin lumyo means the Kachin kind of human, and Myanmar nation also means the Myanmar kind of human. The shortage of the political vocabulary in Myanmar language is also a cause of confusion. The conflicts between the Bama and the non-Bama have been described as the *Lumyo-yey wars* by the indigenous people. The term *lumyo-yey wars* can be translated into *racial wars*. The racial segregation and hatred among the Myanmar ethnic groups is millennium old and can be found in the Myanmar, Mon, Shan, and Rakhine chronicles. One outstanding example is the story of the Bama King Anawrahta (r.1044-1077 CE), the founder of the First Myanmar Empire (1057-1297 CE), and his chief queen Saw Mon Hla who was a Shan princess. The story is forbidden and it is not in the history books anymore. Nonetheless, it is told in the private gatherings and closed door discussions. The story still remains a source of the Bama-Shan racial tension.

One Chin tradition says that the Bama people marauded their land, killed the men and ran away with their women. That is why the Chin started black tattooing the face of their women to look them ugly, with the hope that it will save them from the Bama marauders. This becomes a tradition that exists up to date. You may please go the Chin State and ask about this to the Chin people.

Similarly, the Bama old saying, "If you meet a viper and a Rakhine, kill the Rakhine first,"[13] is still a source of racial hatred. I have come across few Europeans and Americans who know this saying. I was even told[14] that Suu Kyi's father, Bogyoke Aung San, himself uttered

---

[13] I do not know when this saying came to existence, but I guess it was first used in the 1784 war of Bama invasion.

[14] A good number of Rakhine persons from U Seinda generation told me this at different occasions and contexts.

these words upon his frustration at the 1947 Myeybon Conference where the Rakhine people led by Venerable U Seinda[15] called for an independent Arakan, totally opposing Aung San's Union of Burma. Aung San's home town Nat Mauk is in the Central Burma where Burmese pit vipers thrive and where the saying originated.[16] These words are never expressed in public but the words prevail in the private community gatherings. Now, the word 'Rohingya' has become a *taboo*. One can get killed for saying the word "Rohingya'.

Whether the person be a Bama, Rakhine, Shan, Mon, Chin, Kachin, Kaya, Palaung, Pa-O, or Wa, everybody has a racial story. It can be louder at the conflict zones where the armed groups were referred as the Kachin-hsoe (bad Kachin), Karen-hsoe (bad Karen), and Rakhine-hsoe (bad Rakhine), and etc.

3. The Bama Supremacy

The most visible feature of the Bama supremacy is the racial hierarchy where the Bama stands at the top and that justifies the rape as the weapon at the non-Bama regions. There are persistent reports on the use of systematic rape as the weapon in the conflict zones of the Chin, Kachin, Karen, Kaya, Karen,

---

[15] For more information on U Seinda. see Shwe Lu Maung, *The Rakhine State Violence, Vol. 1: the Rakhaing Revolution*, Shahnawaz Khan Publication (USA), 2014

[16] I used to collect pit viper venom when I was stationed at the Magway College in 1969. I have training in the snake handling and anti-venom serum production in my zoology honors research project. I visited Nat Mauk and Aung San's house in that period.

Mon, Rakhine, and Shan areas, and also as punishment in the city detention centers. Some examples are given below.

1. *Statement of the Special Rapporteur on the Situation of Human Rights in Myanmar*, Yangon International Airport, Myanmar, 26 July 2014.
http://www.ohchr.org/EN/NewsEvents/Pages/DisplayNews.aspx?NewsID=14909&LangID=E

2. Dispatches: *Punish Rape in Burma, Not Those Protesting it* by David Scott Mathieson, July 9, 2014.
http://www.hrw.org/news/2014/07/09/dispatches-punish-rape-burma-not-those-protesting-it

3. *License to rape: How Burma's military employs systematic sexualized violence*, Phyu Phyu Sann and Akila Radhakrishnan, March 15, 2012.
http://www.womenundersiegeproject.org/blog/entry/license-to-rape-how-burmas-military-employs-systematic-sexualized-violence

4. *Same Impunity, Same Pattern: Report of Systematic Sexual Violence in Burma's Ethnic Areas*, January 14, 2014.
http://womenofburma.org/same-impunity-same-pattern-report-of-systematic-sexual-violence-in-burmas-ethnic-areas/

5. *Group says Myanmar's army still using rape as weapon of war, with 100 cases since 2011*, January 15, 2014, Associated Press.

http://www.foxnews.com/world/2014/01/15/group-says-myanmar-army-still-using-rape-as-weapon-war-with-100-cases-since/

6. For the reports on the rape as punishment, please see Bertil Lintner, *Outrage*, Review Publishing, Hong Kong, 1989, and the *Statement of the Special Rapporteur on the Situation of Human Rights in Myanmar*, Yangon International Airport, Myanmar, 26 July 2014, which has also been cited earlier.

On the rape, Suu Kyi has expressed her concern at a conference in 2011. Her talk on a video clip can be listened at–
http://nobelwomensinitiative.org/2011/05/aung-san-suu-kyi-on-sexual-violence-in-conflict/

Her emphasis was more on the gender equality but 'rape as the racial violence' or 'weapon in war zone' was not emphasized. However, she did mention the ethnic division as follows.

"Rape is used in my country as a weapon against those who only want to live in peace, who only want to assert their basic human rights, especially in areas of ethnic nationalities. Rape is rife. It is used as a weapon by the armed forces to intimidate the ethnic nationalities and divide our country."

She said these words in an international forum outside Myanmar, but never mentioned within Myanmar. It appears that she downplayed the racial as well as the religious aspects of the Bama and non-Bama conflict. The Kachins and the Chins are all Christians. About

25% of the Karen are estimated to be Christians but almost all members of the Karen National Union (KNU) that is fighting against the Bama government are the Christians. The Karen Buddhists split off from the KNU to form the Democratic Karen Buddhist Army (DKBA) in 1994, after the Bama Buddhist monks lobbied them not to be associated with the Karen Christians. The Rohingyas of the Rakhine State are the Muslims. Therefore, it is hard to totally eliminate the racial and religious aspects of rape as weapon in Myanmar.

The big question is–
Why shall not we openly discuss these thorny and sensitive racial issues?

By keeping these issues suppressed and prohibited, as taboos behind closed doors, we are simply brewing jungle fires, and we are seeing the jungle fires in the Rakhine State, Mandalay, Meiktila, and in all conflict zones around the borders of Myanmar.

In the eyes the world, Suu Kyi is the only qualified Myanmar person to lead Myanmar into openness. When she is silent, conserved, reserved, or calculating at a time of dire need for openness and transparency a legitimate question arises.

Is Suu Kyi a racist?

Since Suu Kyi is working hard to become the Myanmar president the answer is in urgent need. In my attempt to get the answer I again analyze Myanmarism and Myanmar politics, [17] turning every stone that I come across in the hostile terrain of Myanmar.

---

[17] Please see my earlier books on these subjects.

2
Burma or Myanmar?

Daw Suu's country is no doubt a land of conflicts; even the name of the country is in dispute. Daw Suu and her party NLD were advised by the Union Election Commission[18] (Exhibit-2) on June 28, 2012, not to call the country 'Burma' vide the provision of the 2008 Union Constitution, Chapter 1, Section 2, which says "The State shall be known as the Republic of the Union of Myanmar." The advisory note was not only officially dispatched to the NLD head office but it was also published in its full text for the public information.

Daw Suu reportedly defended[19] 'Burma' rebutting the authorities, "I call my country 'Burma' as we did a long time ago. I'm not insulting other people. Because I believe in democracy, I'm sure that I can call it as I like," Well said! The United States of America, Canada, European countries and Australia also like calling 'Burma'. 'Burma' surely is 'English' but not 'Myanmarese'. In my elementary and middle schools in the 1950s, we were taught by the language and history teachers that it was 'Mranmar', a derivative of 'Brahma(r)' and 'Myanmar' is the Bama people corruption of 'Mranmar', just like 'Rangoon' was changed to

---

[18] Myanma Alinn, June 29, 2012, p3
[19] http://www.irrawaddy.org/archives/8282

Exhibit-2
Myanmar Election Commission warned Suu Kyi
that it is Myanmar not Burma on June 28, 2012

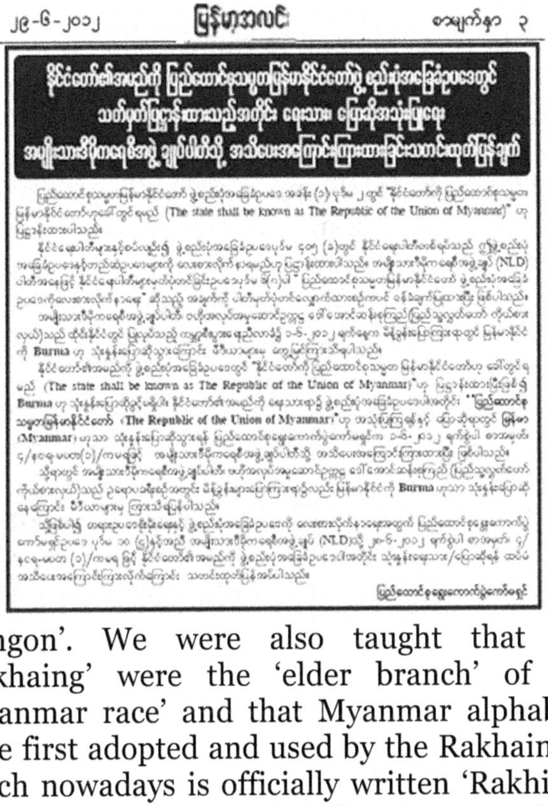

'Yangon'. We were also taught that the 'Rakhaing' were the 'elder branch' of the 'Myanmar race' and that Myanmar alphabets were first adopted and used by the Rakhaing,[20] which nowadays is officially written 'Rakhine'. There was a short period that it was written 'Yakhine' and upon objection from the Rakhine people the authorities officially adopted the spelling 'Rakhine'. I call these linguistic glitches.

---

[20] The Rkhaing (Rakhine) speaks an archaic form of Myanmar dialect but the written language is the same.

In the jungle of linguistic glitches, I am convinced that Myanmar is the original name of Burma, which is believed to be the British version of Bama. On the other hand, it is also possible that 'Burma' is the British corruption of Brahma, which is believed to be the linguistic root of Mranmar. I have faith in my childhood teachers and I believe in what they taught me. If so, the most probable scenario is that the Myanmar people corrupted the English word 'Burma' to 'Bama' because there was no 'Bama' before the British occupation in 1885. The word Bama was found in the history beginning with 'Doe Bama Asi-ayone' (The Association of We-the-Burman) and its slogan 'Thakin-myoh-heh-doe-Bama' (We-Burman-The-Lords) in the second decade of the twentieth century with the beginning of the independence struggle. A person named Kyaw Zaw Aung[21] wrote a good article about the origin of the word 'Myanmar' in the Myanma Ahlin daily newspapers on June 13, 2012. In the stone inscription of Kyansittha's Palace foundation in 1102 CE it was inscribed 'Mirma'; the word is underlined in the clip given below. His presentation strengthened my childhood learning and made me comfortable with the view that 'Myanmar' is historically and politically more acceptable than 'Burma'. Therefore, I will call the country 'Myanmar', her people 'Myanmarese' and her

---

[21] Kyaw Zaw Aung. *"Myanmar" wahara thamaing* (History of the term 'Myanmar), Myanma Ahlin, June 13, 2012, page 9.

national ideology 'Myanmarism'.[22] After all, Daw Suu said, "I'm sure that I can call it as I like." Yes, democracy means freedom of expression.

Exhibit-3
History of the term 'Myanmar'
by Kyaw Zaw Aung
Myanma Alinn June 13, 2012

Before we proceed, as a matter of academic interest, it is worthwhile to mention that Bengal scholars in general believe that the Mrama tribe in Bangladesh and Northern Bengal area is the ancestral root of the today Myanmar people. They believe that Mrama is the Mongolian corruption of Brahma. Their

---

[22] In contrast I used the term 'Burma' and 'Burmese' my earlier book – Burma *Nationalism and Ideology*, University Press Ltd., Dhaka, 1989.

belief tallies with the mythology I was taught in my childhood. In Myanmar traditional cosmology the earth is formed and destroyed and re-formed endlessly in a cyclic manner. At the end of the world ten suns will rise, the earth will be burned and all earthly beings and living organisms will be destroyed. Eventually the heat will cool down and the rain will fall. New soil will appear, generating a sweet aroma and fragrance. The Brahma of the Brahma World get attracted by the fragrance, come down to the earth, taste the earthly essence and lo – they lose their divine power and settle down on earth to become human. When a human dies and if he or she had lived a life abiding Brahma-so-tayar (Laws of Brahma) the human goes back to the Brahma World. Such is the cycle of cosmos and life until one attains Nibban (Nirvana). Now, you know that the Myanmar people are of the divine origin! Quite a good feeling – won't you say so!?

It is in their context of the divine superiority that the Myanmar people look at *'the others'*. In other words, the superiority complex or racism is the central philosophy of Myanmarism.[23]

---

[23] Also see Shwe Lu Maung, *The Price of Silence: Muslim-Buddhist War of Bangladesh and Myanmar – A Social Darwinist's Analysis*, DewDrop Arts & Technology, USA, 2005. This book is all about Myanmarism.

3
Myanmar Imperial Order

**Three kings
at Nay Pyi Taw**

Anawrahta   Bayinnaung   Alaungphaya

Today, Myanmarism derives its legitimacy from its past imperialism. In its cherished concept, the imperialism is an accepted means of unification of the tribes and small national kingdoms into an empire or a greater nation. As of today, it is equated with modern nationhood of the Union of Myanmar. The military rulers selected three most significant kings out of more than one hundred as the source of the 'imperial order' and devolution of state and national legitimacy. They grace and bless Nay Pyi Taw, the nation's capital. Anawrahta started, Bayinnaung glorified, and Alaunphyaya championed the Myanmar Empire.

King Anawrahta (1044-1077 CE) was the first person who, with pragmatism and militarism, institutionalized the Myanmar Way and Myanmar Style.[24]

> The Revival of Myanmarism
> ### 4.1. Myanmar Way and Myanmar Style
> ### Myanmar-hmuu Myanmar-han
> (မြန်မာမှု မြန်မာဟာန်)
>
> See Shwe Lu Maung, *The Price of Silence*, Chapter 4.1

He was also known as Anawrahta Soa. Some scholars believe that Anawrahta is the Myanmar version of Indian Srì Aniruddhadeva or Anuruddha. One of the ten top disciples of Lord Buddha was Venerable Mahathera Anuruddha. He was an Arahat, meaning a Bikkhu who has attained Enlightenment (Nibban). He earned fame for his superhuman magic powers. If Anawrahta is the Myanmar version of Anuruddha he must have adopted this name after his conversion to Buddhism in 1057 CE under the teaching of a Mon monk named Arahan. He also converted all his subjects in the Pagan kingdom into Buddhism and seized Mon Thuwanna Bhumi Tha-hton kingdom to obtain Buddha Three Pitakts. It is very likely that the peoples of Pagan did not call themselves Myanmar at that time. What

---

[24] For more information on Myanmar Way and Myanmar Style, see Shwe Lu Maung, *The Price of Silence: Muslim-Buddhist War of Bangladesh and Myanmar – A Social Darwinist's Analysis*, DewDrop Arts & Technology, USA, 2005.

we know as the Myanmar language in the Myazedi Stone Inscription was visibly introduced only in 1112 CE by Prince Raza Kumar, the son of King Kyansittha (1084-1113 CE). The presence of *Soa*, i.e. Anawrahta Soa, as his last name also suggests his lineage to a pre-Myanmar ethnic group, probably the Pyu. Regardless of his origin, historical evidence indicates that he seeded the foundation of today's Myanmarism.

He regimented his kingdom by assigning military administrative zones. He categorized the villages as the 'ten-zone', 'hundred-zone', etc. A village, which is classified as a ten-zone, has to supply ten soldiers to the king when summoned whereas a hundred-zone village has to supply one hundred soldiers. As such he raised a strong army and founded an empire that is known today as the First Myanmar Empire.[25] Since then he has been the source of Myanmar sovereignty. Every king after him tries to follow his footsteps. Bayinnaung and Alaungphaya came in par with him and recorded as the founder of the Second (1540-1599 CE) and Third (1753-1885 CE) Myanmar Empires, respectively. Please see the maps presented in the coming pages.[26]

---

[25] Daw Mya Sein in her book *Burma*, Oxford University Press; Reprint edition (January 1, 1945), gives a good account of Anawrahta administration. Daw Mya Sein is a Rakhaing and daughter of famous bureaucrat U May Aung, ICS

[26] The historical timeline given are from Sir Arthur P. Phyare, *History of Burma*, London: Trübner & Co., 1883.

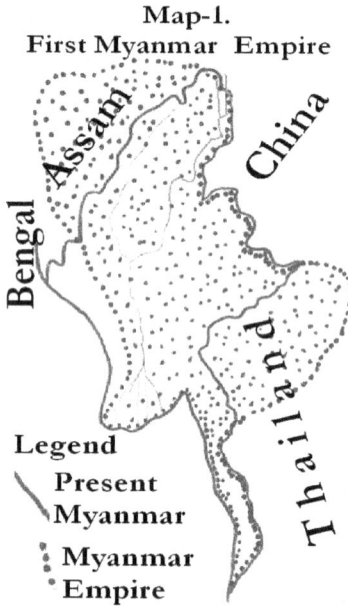

Map-1.
First Myanmar Empire

Legend
Present
Myanmar
Myanmar
Empire

Map-1. The map shows an approximate expansion, in the dotted boundaries, of the First Myanmar Empire (1057-1297 CE), on the top of the present international borders. Rakkhapura was not conquered by King Anawrahta. In the year 1057, King Anawrahta conquered the Mon Kingdom Tha-Hton.

Map-2.
Second Myanmar Empire

Legend
Present
Myanmar

Myanmar
Empire

Map-2. The map shows an approximate expansion, in the dotted boundaries, of the Second Myanmar Empire (1540-1599 CE), in addition to the present international borders. The Second Myanmar Empire did not conquer Rakkhapura, (Kingdom of Arakan); rather it was destroyed by the Rakkhapureans in 1599. Accordingly, the Rakkhapurean king Raza Gri *alias* Salim Shah is known as the Emperor of Pegu, which was the royal seat of the Second Myanmar Empire.

Map-3.
Third Myanmar Empire

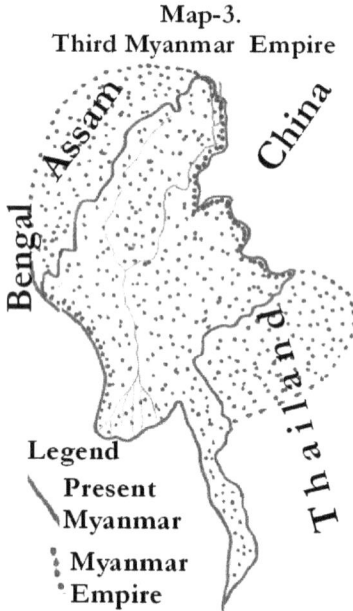

Legend

Present
Myanmar

Myanmar
Empire

Map-3. The map shows an approximate expansion, in the dotted boundaries, of the Third Myanmar Empire (1753-1885 CE), on top of the present international borders. Rakkhapura (Kingdom of Arakan) was conquered by the Myanmar king Bodaw in 1784, just 8 years after the United States of America declared independence. While a new nation was born free in the West my kingdom lost her freedom in the East. Myanmar occupation of Rakkhapura violated the demarcated international boundary agreed by the Rakkhapurean king Mun Khari *alias* Ali Khan (r. 1434-1459 CE) and the Myanmar Ava

King Narapati (r. 1442-1468 CE). Narapati is also known as Thihathu.

Since the days of General Ne Win's rule the aristocrats and official historians called the independent Union of Myanmar the Fourth Myanmar Union. The First, the Second, the Third Myanmar Empires are now labeled as the First, the Second, the Third Myanmar Union. Ne Win's successors Saw Maung and Than Shwe asserted that the Fourth Myanmar Union was founded by Aung San. The devolution of the Myanmar Imperial Order upon the Union of Myanmar is considered Myanmar colonialism and myriads of armed rebellion by the 'federating nations' emerged.[27] The words of the New Mon State Party founder Nai Shwe Kyin[28] are given here as an example.

"Our aim is to reclaim the traditional and historical homeland of the Mon people which was conquered by the Burmese in 1757 and which did not receive its own rights after independence from Great Britain in 1948." Nai Shwe Kyin (1913-2003), founder President of NMSP, founded in 1958.

---

[27] Shwe Lu Maung, *Burma Nationalism and Ideology*, University Press Ltd., Dhaka, 1989. See Chapter 3, Chapter 6.4, and Chapter 7.1.
[28] http://www.nmsp.info/index-eng.php

Exhibit-4

"Our aim is to reclaim the traditional and historical homeland of the Mon people which was conquered by the Burmese in 1757 and which did not receive its own rights after independence from Great Britain in 1948." Nai Shwe Kyin (1913 -2003), founder President of NMSP, founded in 1958.

http://www.nmsp.info/index-eng.php

At the time of writing this book furious battles are being fought between the Kachin Independence Army and the Myanmar forces as per news reported by the Kachin News Group.[29] For more details of the etiology of the armed conflict the reader is recommended to read my book *Burma Nationalism and Ideology*.[30]

---

[29] http://www.kachinnews.com/

[30] Shwe Lu Maung, *Burma Nationalism and Ideology*, University Press Ltd., Dhaka, 1989.

Exhibit-5
The Kachin-Burman War

http://www.kachinnews.com/news/war/2349-burmese-military-suffers-high-casualties-after-a-recent-offensive-against-kia.html

Burmese military suffers high casualties after a recent offensive against KIA

IN WAR · LAST UPDATED ON 36 JULY 2012 · BY KNG ·

Credit: Kachin News Group (KNG)

Myanmar Constitution 2008 mentioned the continuation of its imperial order to the present day situation in its *Preamble*, which is given below.

"Preamble

Myanmar is a Nation with magnificent historical traditions. We, the National people, have been living in unity and oneness, setting up an independent sovereign State and standing tall with pride.

Due to colonial intrusion, the Nation lost her sovereign power in 1885. The National people launched anti-colonialist struggles and National liberation struggles, with unity in strength, sacrificing lives and hence the Nation became an independent sovereign State again on 4th January 1948."

Post 1948 independent Myanmar is supposed to be a republic in which modern norms of human rights reside and prosper. So far, Myanmar has failed to draw a clear demarcation line at 1948, thus creating a situation in which the post-1948 republic is getting dissolved in the toxic deluge of pre-1948 imperial colonialism. Nevertheless, the Myanmar people dwell in their 'magnificent historical traditions', which are duly glorified in the preamble of the 2008 Myanmar Constitution. It is in this context of the *'magnificent historical traditions'* of the First, the Second, and the Third Myanmar Empires that the superiority of the Myanmar people is defined and glorified as a titanic pillar of the Myanmarism.

4
Myanmar National Order

သခင်မျိုး ဟေ့ ဒို့ဗမာ
We Bama The Master Race

Modern Myanmar national order was born in the concept of a master race. The Myanmar independence struggle was brought into force by the We Burman Association or *Dobama Asiayone* in the second decade of the 20th century. Their slogan was "We Bama The Master Race". At that time Bama was Myanmar and Myanmar was Bama. Now, Bama is a national race among the one hundred and thirty five Myanmar races.

In my primary school days in 1950s we were taught that 'Myanmar's origin is at Tagaung'. The rhyme *'Myanmar asa Tagaung ka'*, which means 'Myanmar's origin is at Tagaung' was very popular. We used to sing it in chorus in the history class at the middle school.[31] Myanmar word 'asa' means 'origin' and 'ka' means 'at' in this context. Myanmar words may carry different meanings depending on the context.

The teacher asked, "Myanmar asa?"

We happily answered in chorus, "Tagaung ka".

Teacher, "Good! Now sing Myanmar asa Tagaung ka."

---

[31] From Standard 5 to 7 was the middle school.

We sang loud until the next door class teacher came and complained. Such fun we had with *'Myanmar asa Tagaung ka'*.

Sadly though, in the middle of 1960s, that history was erased and it became 'Myanmar asa Anawrahta ka', meaning 'Myanmar begins with Anawrahta' in 1044 CE. We learned that pre-Anawrahta history was so much shady that it became a matter of embarrassment to the historians and research-less nation; the historians suggested a change of the nation's origin. General Ne Win, a great fan of King Anawrahta, found it quite agreeable. What about the people at large? Most of them did not know and those who knew did not care. Job and food were more important to them. Who cares about something that happened more than one thousand years ago?

Exhibit-6
Emblem of
the Association of
Myanmar Archaeologists
Please note the Srivatsa
symbol

Then, was Tagaung real or myth? It was real, not a myth. Postings in 2009 by the Association of Myanmar Archaeologists (AOMAR)[32] shed some light into the pre-Bagan[33] era and gave substance to the legendary verbal and written records. The AOMAR wrote:

Exhibit-7
Myanmar Archaeologists
at work at Tagaung excavation 2009
Photo credit: AOMAR

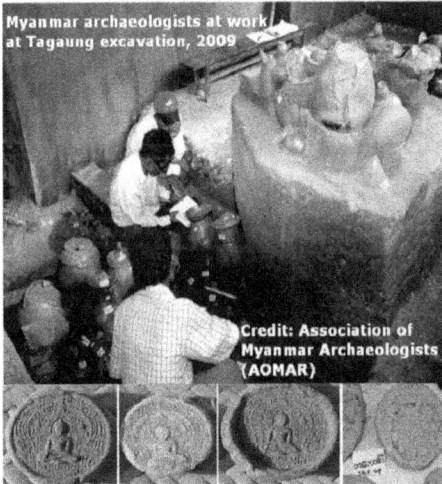

"Tagaung and Bagan are closer to the Ayeyarwaddy than Halin, Maingmaw, Waddi or Beikthano. While the west wall of both is currently near the Ayeyarwaddy, each may once have been farther from the bank and the

---

[32] http://aomar.wordpress.com/2008/12/04/excarvation-at-tagaung/
[33] Earlier Bagan was written Pagan. Since 1988 Myanmar officially use Bagan replacing Pagan.

threat of flood. At Bagan, Daw Thin Gyi concluded from aerial photographs that the west wall has been gradually lost to the Ayeyarwaddy through erosion and flood. A jutting out of the river at the village of Myit Khe ('lower portion') north of Bagan also supports its gradual eastward shift. Beyond this, however, comparison weakens, for Bagan's setting may have obviated the need for fortification on the immediate east while the ecology and location of Tagaung may have required it. The site's strategic position on the Yunnan frontier is evident in the array of Tagaung artefacts attributed to its use by the 11th century AD Anawrahta as part of his east flank fortification. Ores may additionally explain Anawrahta's interest in Tagaung, with silver continuing in use at Bagan for land and slave purchases. Tagaung afforded access to the silver mines of Bawdwin and Yadanatheingyi at Namtu in around Mogok. It is also via Mogok and the Shweli and Taping (Tabein) rising in the uplands that Tagaung linked to Yunnan via Muse and Bhamo. Other resources including jade, copper and iron were reachable by the Meza and Uru watercourses to the north and northwest."

Obviously the people of Myanmar has marched milleniums towards a nationhood but their journey is yet to continue without an end. In view of the fact that 'future is more important than the past' the people of Myanmar should focus on the future than the past. Today, one hundred and thirty five officially recognized national races plus a number of unofficial races such as the Rohingya and people of China and Indian origin are bogged down in civil war, racial-religious dicrimination and more seriously ethnic cleansing.

Map-4. Showing some kingdoms of pre-Bagan period

Myanmar archaelogical excavations at various places, some settlements dating back to mesolithic and neolithic era, indicate human settlements since antiquity in the land now we call Myanmar, see the Map-4, p 35. So many kingdoms and civilizations must have appeared and disappeared that Myanmar now can proudly list one hundred and thirty five races[34] and also furiously denies existence of unlisted or neglected races.

If you look at the map-4 given here it is tempting to reason that Bagan was a meeting point of the pre-Bagan people since it was a central point in geographical consideration. It was probable that it became a geo-political center in course of time and a new kingdom and nation emerged in the cycles of war and peace.

On the other hand its overemphasis of the races based on the Myanmar traditional term 'Lu-Myo' meaning 'kind of human' is proving to be counter-productive in the process of building a modern *State*. These days the nations are going to a 'state beyond the nation state', as we evidence the emergence of the United States of America as early as in 1776, the European Union (EU) in 1993, the Association of the South East Asian Nation (ASEAN) Community to take the office in 2015, and the South Asian Association of Regional Cooperation (SAARC) formed in 1985. Therefore, we shall try to formulate a new

---

[34] http://www.myanmar.com/gov/tourist/pop.html on May 09, 2001.

national order in Myanmar to be in harmony with changing politico-economical atmosphere in the globe.

Present Myanmar national order is a form of racism since its nationalism and citizenship is absolutely confined to the 135 national races who are considered to be indigenous prior to 1823 CE, the year before the First Anglo-Burman war. All others are alienated, discriminated and deprived of rights as observed in the typical case of the Rohingya Muslims who are considered non-Myanmar regardless of the credible evidence of their aboriginality.[35] Myanmar official classification of the national races is given below.

"Population and National Races of Myanmar"[36]

Myanmar is a union of many nationalities as many as 135 groups, with their own languages and dialects. The term Myanmar embraces all nationalities: the Bamar, the Chin, the Kachin, the Kayah, the Kayin, the Mon, the Rakhine and the Shan. Each of them belongs to one of the three major racial groups: the Mon-khmers, the Tibeto-Bamars and the Thai-Shans. According to the statistics of 1998-99, the population of the country is estimated at 47.25 million and the population growth rate is 1.84 percent. Males constitute 23.46 million, forming 49.66

---

[35] Shwe Lu Maung, *The Rakhine State Violence*, Vol. 2: The Rohingya, Shahnawaz Khan Publication (USA), 2014.
[36] http://www.myanmar.com/gov/tourist/pop.html on May 09, 2001

percent and females constitute 23.79 million, forming 50.34 percent. It is expected that population will reach 50 million by the year 2000."[37]

Table-1. List of the official Myanmar National Races

(A) Kachin National Races.

1. Kachin	5. Gaw-ri	9. Ra-wom
2. Hsa-gon	6. Sa-U	10. La-shi (Lar-chit)
3. Da-laung	7. Du-rin	11. A-zee (Zaing-wa)
4. Ting-hpaw	8. Ma-Gu (Kaw-paw)	12. Li-hsu

(B) Kayah National Races.

1. Kayah	4. Gai-kho	7. Manu-manaw (Kaw-yaw-Mo)
2. Za-yim	5. Gai-tha	8. Yin-talai
3. Kam-yam (Pa-daung)	6. Pa-yai (Ka-yaw)	9. Yin-baw

(C) Kayin National Races.

1. Kayin	5. Sa-hwaw (Sa-kaw)	9. Maw-nay-bwa
2. Kayin-hpyu	6. Tahlay-pwar	10. Moe-pwar
3. Palay-kee (Palay-chi)	7. Pa-ku	11. Sho (Poe)

---

[37] The 2014 Myanmar census reported 51 millions.

4. Mon-kayin (Sahpyu-kayin)	8. Twe	12. Pa-O (Paung-tha)

(D) Chin National Races.

1. Chin	18. Zar-htaung	35. Ma-kan
2. Mai-htai (Ka-the)	19. Zo-hton	36. Ma-tu
3. Salai	20. Zo-pay	37. Miram (a) Mara
4. Lin-kaw (Lu-shai)	21. Zo	38. Mi-tai
5. Kha-mi	22. Zan-hnyat (Zan-ni-yam)	39. Mwin
6. Auwa-khami	23. Ta-paung	40. Lu-shai (Lu-shay)
7. Khaw-no	24. Ti-dim(Te-dim)	41. Lay-myo
8. Khaung-kho	25. Tay-zan	42. Lin-te
9. Kaung-saing-chin	26. Tai-chun	43. Lauk-tu
10. Khwar-lim	27. Ta-doe	44. Lai
11. Khun-li (a) Sim	28. Htaw-yi	45. Lai-zo
12. Gan-te	29. Dim	46. Par-kim (a) Mro
13. Gway-te	30. Dai (Yin-du)	47. Hwarl-ngo
14. Ngun	31. Naga	48. Ah-nu
15. Hsi-zan	32. Tan-du	49. Ah-nan
16. Hsin-htan	33. Mar-yin	50. Ah-sho-chin (Myay-pyan)
17. Saing-zan	34. La-nam	51. Raung-tu

(E) Bamar National Races.

1. Bamar	4. Yaw	7. Ga-nan
2. Dawei	5. Ra-thein	8. Hsa-lon
3. Myeik	6. Ga-du(khon-tu)	9. Hpon(Hpun)

(F) Mon National Races.

1. Mon *(Note: only one. A lonely race, it is.)*

(G) Rakhine National Races.

1. Rakhine	4. Daing-net	7. Thet
2. Kaman	5. Mra-mar-Gyi	
3. Khamee	6. Myo	

(H) Shan National Races

1. Shan	13.Tai-khamti	25. Wa
2. Yun (La-O)	14. Gon (Khun)	26. Aik
3. Kwi	15. Taung-yoe	27. Pa-O (Taung-thu)
4. Hpyin	16. Danu	28. Tai-Lwoi
5. Tha-O	17. Pa-laung	29. Tai-Liam
6. Sa-naw	18. Myaung-zee	30. Tai-Lon
7. Si-lay	19. Yin-kyar	31. Tai-lay
8. In	20. Yin-net	32. Mong-thar
9. Son (Hsan)	21. Tai-kaik	33. Mong-maw

10.Kha-mu	22. Tai-khun	34. Inn-tha
11. Kay (Ah-kha)	23. La-hu	
12. Ko-kang	24. Lwai-la	

Despite the diversity and geographic separation the national groups share with each other a wide variety of social customs. Blessed with a favourable climate and inhabited by a happy, creative peoples, Myanmar culture on the whole is indigenous." (End of quotes from http://www.myanmar.com/gov/tourist/pop.html, on May 09, 2001).

Diagram-1. Myanmar racial hierarchy inverted pyramid

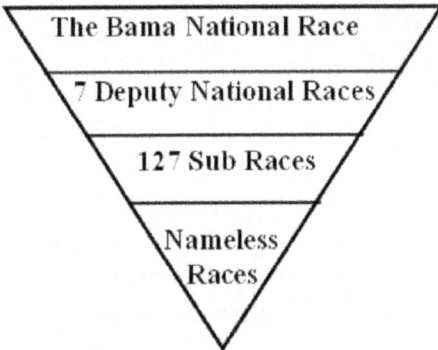

The Bama National Race

7 Deputy National Races

127 Sub Races

Nameless Races

Myanmar officially highlights that "each of them belongs to one of the three major racial groups: the Mon-khmers, the Tibeto-Bamars and the Thai-Shans," and they are the Myanmar citizens; all others are aliens with no rights in the country. Therefore Myanmar national order is a Burmese variety of racial ethnocentric colonialism, in which the larger ethnic group rules the smaller ones with the sovereign power emanating from the Bama National Race. It exists and functions as an inverted pyramid that is illustrated in the word diagram. Classification of the national races is adopted from the Myanmar government official web site, myanmar.com[38]

The principle of the Myanmar national races constitutes the Myanmar racial hierarchy[39] that is illustrated in the Diagram-1.

The Bama National Race: The Bama National Race constitutes the First Class Citizens and is the ruling class and colonial masters. Myanmar.com lists a total of 9 sub races in this class. They constitute 40% of the total Myanmar population, 49 millions in 2004. Their powerhouse is known as the Burma Proper that consists of 7 administrative Divisions.

Seven Deputy National Races: The Second Class Citizens or the Deputy Ruling Races are made up of seven major national races namely, 1. Kachin National Races (with

---

[38] http://www.myanmar.com/gov/tourist/pop.html, as of November, 2004. This web page was not found on August 21, 2014. Also see http://en.wikipedia.org/wiki/List_of_ethnic_groups_in_Burma
[39] Also see Shwe Lu Maung, *The Price of Silence: Muslim-Buddhist War of Bangladesh and Myanmar – A Social Darwinist's Analysis*, DewDrop Arts & Technology, USA, 2005, p 159.

12 sub races), 2. Kaya National Races (with 9 sub races), 3. Kayin National Races (with 12 sub races), 4. Chin National Races (with 51 sub races), 5. Mon National Races (with no sub race), 6. Rakhine National Races, (with 7 sub races), and 7. Shan National Races (with 34 sub races). Populations of the Kachin, the Kaya, the Kayin, the Chin, the Mon, the Rakhine, and the Shan vary from 2 to 7 millions and in total they together constitute about 40% of the total Myanmar population. The new constitution empowers them as the autonomous states, with limited power to formulate their culture and local administration.

Sub Races: The Third Class Citizens are constituted by the 127 small sub races, which make up about 15% of the total Myanmar population. Each of these sub races is less than 0.5% of the total population. They virtually have no political clout. Even if Myanmar becomes an ideal democratic country their votes will not make any change in the Myanmar racial *status quo*. Some of them such as Khamee, Pa-O, Pa-Laung and Kokang are honored with Self-Administration Zone or Division.

Nameless Races: Fourth Class Citizens are classified as the immigrants from India sub continent and China. They make up about 5% of the total Burmese population and are known as the Kala and the Tayut respectively. They are classified as the guest-citizens. The Muslims of the Rakhine State strongly dispute this classification and they identify themselves as the Rohingya, natives of Arakan. Such other Indian descendants as the Sikh, the Gurkha, the Bengali, the Tamil, etc. stay very low profile. The Chinese people are wealthy, educated and live wisely by simply minding their business, without indulging in politics.

More notably, the smaller 'national races' object the racial hierarchal designation. For example, the mizzima.com on January 13, 2014, reported[40] the objection of the Kayan people against the racial designation. In the government classification Kayan[41] is written Kam-yam or Pa-daung (see Table-1 (B) Kayah National Races). The excerpt of the news is given below.

"Members of the Kayan ethnic group have objected to being described as a sub-group of the Kayah in the forthcoming national census, saying the designation is degrading.

The objection was outlined in a statement issued by seven Kayan organisations on January 11.

"The Kayan are a separate ethnic group and we are not subordinate to the Kayah," Colonel Saw Lwin, the joint secretary (1) of the Kayan New Land Party told Mizzima on January 12.

---

[40] http://www.mizzima.com/mizzima-news/ethnic-issues/item/10812-kayan-object-to-designation-in-planned-census. Last accessed on August 18, 2014.
[41] For more information on Kayan or Pa-daung, see http://en.wikipedia.org/wiki/Kayan_people_(Burma)

"By categorizing us in this way the government has created dissention;[42] it is as if our ethnic group is regarded as small and unimportant," Col Saw Lwin said."

However, totally ignoring the racial ethnocentric colonial characters, but in a view of romantic nationalism, the 2008 Myanmar Constitution in its 'Preamble' inscribes peace and harmony of the national races as below.

"We, the National people, drafted this Constitution of the Republic of the Union of Myanmar in accord with the Basic Principles and Detailed Basic Principles laid down by the National Convention.
We, the National people, firmly resolve that we shall:
- steadfastly adhere to the objectives of non-disintegration of the Union, nondisintegration of National solidarity, and perpetuation of sovereignty;
- stalwartly strive for further burgeoning the eternal principles namely justice, liberty, equality and perpetuation of peace and prosperity of the National people;
- uphold racial equality, living eternally in unity fostering the firm Union Spirit of true patriotism;
- constantly endeavour to uphold the principles of peaceful co-existence among

---

[42] The 'dissention' is the original spelling in the news report. In the United States it is commonly spelled 'dissension'.

nations with a view to having world peace and friendly relations among nations.

DO HEREBY ADOPT this Constitution of the Republic of the Union of Myanmar through a nation-wide referendum on the Tenth day of Kasone Waning, 1370 M.E. (The Twenty-Ninth day of May, 2008 A.D.)"

In the constitution please note that it is 'We, the National people, but it is not 'We, the people'.

It is understandable that 'from-Burma-to-Myanmar' is an attempt to unite the divided races into one nation under the name of Myanmar. The Bama race is trying to compromise by descending a one-step down, with a gesture that the Bama is just one of many and equal to all and one. On the other hand Aung San Suu Kyi insists on calling it Burma and Bama. In reality, the nomenclature, Burma or Myanmar, does not change the racial philosophy of the Myanmar national order, which is strengthened by the Citizenship Act of Burma 1982, alienating all the people who do not fit into the classification of the official Myanmar national races.[43] The biggest problem is that 134 *national races,* (that is [135 minus Bama]), insist that they are neither Bama nor Myanmar.

---

[43] For more information on the Citizenship Act of Burma 1982, see Shwe Lu Maung, *The Price of Silence: Muslim-Buddhist War of Bangladesh and Myanmar – A Social Darwinist's Analysis*, DewDrop Arts & Technology, USA, 2005, pp 235 &250, and Shwe Lu Maung, *The Rakhine State Violence*, Vol. 2: The Rohingya, Shahnawaz Khan Publication (USA), 2014, Chapter 5.

In light of modern science, the racial categories and classifications are obsolete and unscientific. Especially, the most modern science of molecular biology, with clarity and precision of genomic sequences, has demonstrated, beyond doubt, that humankind is one.[44] Therefore, the concept of race is anti-humanism as well as anti-humanity. So far, apart from the argument of "Burma or Myanmar" Suu Kyi has offered no solution to the Myanmar imperial racial hierarchy.

---

[44] See Shwe Lu Maung, *The Rakhine State Violence*, Vol. 2: The Rohingya, Shahnawaz Khan Publication (USA), 2014.

5
Myanmar Socio-Political Order

If we were to accept the relationship of man, society and state is a 'Social Contract' as discussed by Jean Jacques Rousseau, in 1762, we need to understand the basic norms of Myanmar society in order to apprehend the forces that shape the 'Myanmar Social Contract' today.

There was effective decentralization in the Myanmar royal administration and a village headman was an independent administrator as along as he remained loyal to the King. He ruled the village with an informal council of the elders. In every village there was, and still is, a 'village-hall' known as 'rwa-lay-zayat', which literally means a 'village-center-open-house'. It is a building with a roof and a floor without walls but one side of the building will have mini-walls about three-feet high from the floor. This corner is meant for the headman and the elders. The village-hall is also a guest house. The travelers and guests are housed there. It is also a place of ceremonies such as weddings, monk-ordaining of the boys,[45] ear-holing of the girls, Dhamma Recital to drive out the demons from the village and many others. In the evening, the village headman and the elders, - men and women- assembled

---

[45] It is the duty of the Buddhist parents to ordain the sons and to ear-hole the daughters. These ceremonies are done with pomp and fair, entire village and even friends and relatives from far away come to the ceremonies.

there and they will have pots of plain tea, plates of pickled tea salad (laphat-thut) and sand-roasted shell-on peanuts. They will hold meetings or simply discuss and chat. Every villager, man or women, young or old, monk or lay, can be there and participate in the discussions and arguments with no restriction. The headman makes the decision with majority votes and elders' approval. Every matter and every issue of the village is discussed there. Weddings were settled with parental consent. If a boy and a girl eloped the elders will mediate to reach a parental consent. A rowdy youth will be disciplined. Festivals are organized. Tax to be paid to the king will be discussed. The first day of the plowing[46] season is determined. The village elders served as the electoral college and the Crown appointed the village headman. It became hereditary in many cases.

I have been to a number of such 'village parliaments' in the villages of Western and Central Myanmar. The *village parliamentary* tradition was exploited by the British rulers by giving more power to the headman in tax collection. I learned about the glory and power of a village headman, popularly known as

---

[46] The plowing or paddy growing season begins with plowing of the land by a most senior village citizen. It is a big occasion of fun fair, even the Abbots, senior monks, student monks and novices will be there. Young boys and girls reaching aging age, thirteen and above, to plow and plant the saplings will be introduced and honored. In the good old days it was the king who would plow the land with oxen or buffaloes in his royal paddy field and thus launched the paddy growing season. Only after him the village plowing ceremonies followed. This tradition probably is universal since the time immemorial but I believe in Myanmar it was strengthened by King Ŝuddhodana's meticulous practice of the Plowing Ceremony. He was the father of Gautama Buddha.

Rwathugyi-min or just Thugyi-min from my revolutionary leader Bo Gri Kra Hla Aung[47] who was a son of a celebrated and decorated Thugyi-min[48] of the British Era.

The 'village-hall' administration system that I value as the 'village parliaments' existed since the days of pre-Awarahta Bagan.[49] In the later days of post-Anawrahta Pagan a form of royal council known as *Hluttaw* composed of the princes was formed by King Htilominlo (r. 1211 to 1235 CE) and commissioned to function on behalf of the king in taxation and administrative affairs. It is also said that the Konbaung Dynastic kings practiced *Hluttaw* in an extending form. In the post-1948 Myanmar Hluttaw is considered as the origin of the modern parliament and hence the parliament is called *Hluttaw* in Myanmar language. Literally, it means *the Royal Representation*; *Hlutt* means represented and *Taw* stands for royal. In the days of the monarchy Hluttaw represented the king, but not the people.

Prime Minister U Nu, the only legitimate head of the government in Myanmar, tried to build his Buddhistic democracy on the foundation of the village democracy, but his effort was frustrated by the rampant civil war that destroyed many villages and displaced millions of farmers. His national

---

[47] Shwe Lu Maung *alias* Shahnawaz Khan, *Arakanese Student and Youth Movement Bo Gri Kra Hla Aung (1910-1995)*, Arakanpost, Issue 4, May 2004. http://shwelumaung.org/publications/series3.pdf

[48] Two of my mother's cousins and my paternal great-uncle were the hereditary Rwathugyis.

[49] Bagan is the new version of spelling of Pagan since 1988.

development program known as the '*pyitawtha* (happy-land) planning' had a component of rural development program that actively involved the villagers and farmers. His plan was to start a social-welfare society beginning with the village. Ideally, it still sounds good to me. I cherish my belief that had U Nu been given a chance he would have developed a meaningful democracy in Myanmar.

In the days of General Ne Win's rule the centralization of the administration and indoctrination of the villagers with his 'Burmese Way to Socialism' effectively wiped out the 'village parliament'. The Rwathugyi and elders system was replaced with the Village Administrative Council and its members were selected by the Burmese Socialist Programme Party (BSPP). In 1970s the villages crumbled down with bad management, corruption, and weakened economy, which were compounded by the weight of growing population. The village administration and management were so bad under the Burmese Way to Socialism that agricultural output dropped drastically and even famine set in 1977 and 1978. By the early 1980s the village infrastructure was nothing but rubble and Myanmar imploded. This eventually led to the outbreak of the bloody 1988 August uprising that dislodged General Ne Win of the 'Founder Generation'[50] and his old guards of the 'Hero-Generation'

---

[50] For the 'founder and hero generations' see Shwe Lu Maung, *Burma Nationalism and Ideology*, University Press Ltd., Dhaka, 1989, Chapter 8.4.

and brought in the military commanders of the post-independent generation and Aung San Suu Kyi into the arena.

Photo-1
Senior General Saw Maung
at a press conference
July 5, 1989
Photo credit: MNA

No matter what political changes may occur the pagodas remain standing tall and monasteries still ring out the wooden and bamboo bells at the dawn in every village. The boys are ordained and the girls are ear-holed with big celebrations. The festivals are still on and the plowing ceremony survives the Burmese Way to Socialism. More, the 'village halls' still exist in many places. It is this Myanmar Way and Myanmar style of life or 'Myanmar-hmuu Myanmar-han'[51] that the Senior General Saw Maung planned to revive and make it the foundation of a new Myanmar when Senior General Saw Maung declared, "I will rule the country according to the *Lauka-thara Pyo,*" in the aftermath of the 1990 election.

Here are some quotations of Sr. General Saw Maung (1928-1997), Myanmar's first 5-star general, a soldier-ruler-philosopher, who

---

[51] See Shwe Lu Maung *alias* Shahnawaz Khan, *The Price of Silence Muslim-Buddhist War of Bangladesh and Myanmar, A Social Darwinist's Analysis*, DewDrop Art & Technology, USA, 2005, Chapter 4.1.

paved the way to the modern Myanmarism. The photo of Sr. Gen. Saw Maung given here is by MNA, the Ministry of Information, on the occasion of his press conference at the Ministry of Defence Guest House, on July 05, 1989.

"Our military science is more advanced than political science."

"People told me to settle the matters by negotiation. I am a soldier, not a politician. There is no negotiation in military science."

"I will rule the country according to the *Lauka-thara Pyo.*"

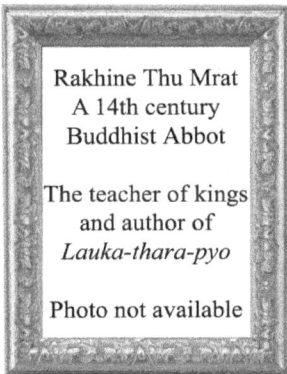

Rakhine Thu Mrat
A 14th century
Buddhist Abbot

The teacher of kings
and author of
Lauka-thara-pyo

Photo not available

Photo-2

The core The *Lauka-thara-pyo*[52] or 'Essence of the World' is based on the Theravada Buddhism. Hence the Theravada Buddhism or 'Elder's Doctrine' is the *prima materia* of the teaching. It is a manual written in verses before or around 1327 CE by a Rakhine[53] Buddhist Bikkhu, known as Rakhine Thu Mrat or Rakhine Holy Man, to teach his students. It was a summary of his teachings. He was the teacher of King Mun Hti (r.1279-1385 CE, Laung Krut Dynasty). King Min Hti entrusted him with the education of three Burmese (Thet

---

[52] Lauka-thara-pyo text, history and biography of Rakhine Thu Mrat are based on the publication' Laukatharapyo' presented and explained by Min Thuu Wun, Linn Oo Tara Literature, Yangon, 1996.
[53] Also spelled 'Rakhaing'.

or Chakma)[54] princes namely Saw Son, Saw Pru, and Saw Tu. They were the sons of King Lyin Saw who was the king of the Chakma (*Thet*).[55] His kingdom Thayet or Thet Yet, meaning the Chakma Province, was seized by the Rakhine King Mun Hti as the Chakma people marauded the Rakhine border villages. Today, the City of Thayet is at the border of central and lower Myanmar. King Lyin Saw and his family were taken to Rakhine while the Rakhine Minister Razasithu Thungran was charged as the Governor of Thayet. Rakhine King Mun Hti was famous for his honesty and promise-keeping (please see the Appendix-1: Mun Hti). He looked after King Lyin Saw and his family well, thus giving good opportunity for the young Myanmar princes to pursue education. (Note: Even though the historians refer to them as the Myanmar princes their first name *Saw,* which is the last name of their father, indicates that they were not Myanmar, but most probably had the Pyu lineage. Remember the names of earlier generations of Pagan kings in pre-Anawrahta era - Pyu Saw

---

[54] Chakma (သက်မ) and *Thet* (သက်). Our Rakhine chronicles tell us that a king of Vārānasi (Banares, Northern India) came and lived as a hermit in Northern Arakan. One *Hsatma* (သမ) happened to drink the water that was contaminated with his urine and later gave birth to a human boy. The boy became the founder king of Rakkhapura in the name of Marayu. The word *Hsatma* is wrongly interpreted as a doe in modern Rakhine dialect. Please see Sir Arthur Phyare's *History of Myanmar*, Trübner & Co, London, 1883, p43. I believe the *Hsatma* actually was a Chakma woman who gave birth to a boy through her union with the hermit king. Our chroniclers hid this act of the hermit.

[55] Also see Shwe Lu Maung, *The Rakhine State Violence*, Vol. 2: The Rohingya, Shahnawaz Khan Publication (USA), 2014, pp 89-90.

Hti, Hti Min Yin, Yin Min Pike, Pike Thay Lay, Thay Lay Kyuw, Kyuw Du Rit? The father's last name becomes the child's first name! It is interesting to see that Saw Tu later became King of Ava with the title of Sao Swa Ke. '*Sao*' is a Shan title and '*Saw*' today is a Karen title!).

In the days of Rakkhapura[56] dynasties the Buddhist monasteries were the universities, designed after the ancient Taxila,[57] which was the biggest university established by Emperor Asoka in western India, now Pakistan. Traditionally, sixteen subjects, including the science of war and Buddhism, were taught to the children of nobles and kings, regardless of sex, in a Buddhist University. Rakhine Thu Mrat was the head monk, or Professor and President, of such a university. When the three princes grew up they became dukes (Myo Hsar) of Myin Sai Myo, Pyi Myo, and Amyint Myo respectively. Later Amyint Myo Hsar Saw Tu (Taraphya Saw Ke) was elected by the ministers and nobles to the throne of Ava in the name of King Sao Swa Ke (r.1367-1404 CE), at the death of the founding King Thadoe Minphya (r.1364-1367 CE). He was elected on the merit that he was a descendant of Pagan Dynasty (1044-1279 CE) and Shan Dynasty (1298-1364 CE). The interlude between the end of Pagan

---

[56] Also spell 'Rakhapura' but 'Rakkhapura' is more relevant spelling for the original Pali spelling and pronunciation.

[57] Takṣhaśhilā, See http://en.wikipedia.org/wiki/Taxila. As per Rakhine traditions the University was established by Emperor Asoka.

Dynasty and the beginning of Shan dynasty is due to the Mongol Chinese Emperor Kubali Khan's occupation of Myanmar.

On the 16th year of his reign, King Sao Swa Ke invited his aging teacher Rakhine Thu Mrat to his kingdom. He worshipped and honored him with the title of *Maha Thingha Raza,* which means *Great Lord Sanga*. Thus *'Lauka-thara-pyo'* reached Myanmar from Rakkhapura and became a royal handbook of the Myanmar Kings as well. It is then that the Rakhine and the Myanmar merged into a common written heritage of cultural norms, and royal administrative philosophy. It was a source of unity between the two historically hostile peoples - the Rakhine and the Bama. It was the first time since 1784 that the Bama admitted *'Maha Thingha Raza'* was none other than *'Rakhine Thu Mrat'* erasing the cause of a 200-year dispute. As a matter of fact, there are many Rakhine descendents in the area of Mandalay, Mun Gwan, and Meiktila of the central Burma because the Burmese kings brought in more than 250,000 Rakhine captives and conscripts in the period from 1784 to 1824 CE. I have a number of *Mandalaythar* (sons of Mandalay) friends who confided me that they had Rakhine blood. In Myanmar society, a *mixed blood* is a disgrace.[58] People hide it the best they can. It is racism. I suspect Saw Maung, a *Mandalaythar*, was of a Rakhine descent.   He had typical Rakhine

---

[58] Please note Suu Kyi's sons shun Myanmar.

characteristics, such as honoring of Rakhine Thu Mrat and having hot temperament and alcoholism! He died of alcoholism that complicated his diabetes.

The junta's announcement to rule the nation in accordance with the *Lauka-thara-pyo* strategically refreshes not only the golden era of Ava but also pacifies the hostility between the two historical rivals. This pacification is so crucial because 30% of the fighting force of the Myanmar armed forces, that is approximately 150,000 in the present strength of 500,000, is made up of the Rakhine youths. The only way the Myanmar armed forces can be broken up is to split off the Rakhine loyalty. With full understanding of this vital tactical issue, the leaders of the armed forces made a radical move to cement and strengthen the Rakhine loyalty.

Introduction of the *Lauka-thara-pyo* as the nation's ruling formula and the junta's due acknowledgement of its author, Rakhine Thu Mrat, as the teacher of the Myanmar kings was a great success. Also remember that Myanmar Ava King Sao Swa Ke was a Tagaung and Pyu origin with a Shan title who revered a Rakhine teacher. This surely is the solidification of the Myanmar national races. This is the craftiest move made by the Myanmar military junta. A modern edition of the *Lauka-thara-pyo* was published with an authoritative interpretation and explanation by none other than Min Thuu Wun (Sayagyi U Wun) who is a *guru*, i.e. more than a professor, of Myanmar literature, a pioneer of modern Myanmar, and a patriot decorated with the national honors of *Wunna Kyaw Htin* and *Thiri Pyanchi*.

Beyond doubt, the Rakhines were effectively incorporated into Myanmarism. For those Rakhines who accepted the defeat of 1784 and simply prayed to get a slice of sympathetic cake it was a blessing whereas it was the most lethal blow to a Rakhine rebel who fought for self-determination. Myanmar observers will notice that the Rakhine rebellion did not gain any momentum in 1988 and onwards despite severe oppression by Senior General Saw Maung and his State Law and Order Restoration Council (SLORC). A fresh national solidarity was brought about by that soldier known as Sr. General Saw Maung. General Ne Win tried to become a philosopher, but turned out to be a brute. On the contrary, Sr. General Saw Maung came in as a brute, but turned out to be a philosopher. The *Lauka-thara-pyo* no doubt is the skeleton of Buddhist political ideology. By adopting it as the ruling philosophy Sr. General Saw Maung gave the Myanmar military junta new impetus in the 21st century.[59]

---

[59] Some parts of Senior General Saw Maung and *Lauka-thara-pyo* have been mentioned in my book- Shwe Lu Maung *alias* Shahnawaz Khan, *The Price of Silence Muslim-Buddhist War of Bangladesh and Myanmar, A Social Darwinist's Analysis*, DewDrop Arts & Technology, USA, 2005, Chapter 4.7.

Diagram-2
Lauka thara pyo
opening verse with my translation

၁॥ ကြားပိမ့်သူမြတ်၊ အများမှတ်စိမ့်॥

ဟိတဿိက၊ သြဝါဒဖြင့်

ဆုံးမပေးတွေ၊ နားဝင်စေလော॥

နေသို့ ထင်ရှား၊ ဘုရား တရား သံဃာ

ရတနာထွတ်ထား၊ မြတ်သုံးပါးကို

ဦးဖျားထိပ်ထက်၊ အမြဲရွက်၍

စုံမက် သဒ္ဓါ ကြည်စေမင်း॥ ॥

လှိုင်းသူမြတ်	Rakhaing Thu Mrat
လောကာသာရပျို့	Lauka thara pyo
မင်းသုဝဏ်	Min Thuu Wun
၇င့်ဆိုရှင်းလင်းသည်။	presents with explanations

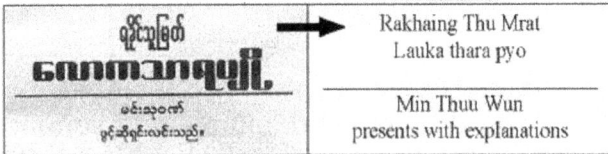

Lauka-thara-pyo, with its fifty five verses, is more of ethic, duty and responsibility than ideological or philosophical. Therefore, it is a teaching of law and order. However, the ethic, duty and responsibility it taught are based upon the pre-Buddhist social order and Theravada Buddhist Laws. Thus, it represents Myanmar way of life. Its style of presentation known as 'pyo' is a very powerful poetic literature and the first of its kind in Myanmar literature. In other words Rakhine Thu Mrat invented 'pyo' form of the Myanmar poems, Diagram-2.

Rakhine Thu Mrat: Laukathara Pyo, Openning Verse, Diagram-2, Part 1, Verse 1, my translation

1. Thu Mrat, shall speak,
So people may learn;
This is a beneficial teaching;
Give ear with due attention.
Brilliant as the sun are the Buddha,
The Dhamma, and the Sangha.
Always carry these jewels
On the apex and cherish them
With serene mind and heart.

It is easy to recite, remember and understand due its plain, simple and common words; even an illiterate can understand it. It is composed of three parts. The part one highlights the ethic of the general populace which is made up of four classes, namely the royal (king, king's employees including soldiers), the *ponna* (Brahmin or intellectual), the well-to-do's (traders or business community) and the commoners (workers and farmers). The second part put emphasis on the ruler whereas the third part focuses on the *ponna*.

There is no question that *Lauka-thara-pyo* sets the framework of the Myanmar social order. Its Part-1, general ethic, is composed of twenty two verses(#1-22) and advises to respect and obey the parents, teachers, king and rulers, and the elders. It also advises to abide by the five precepts – avoidance of 'killing', 'stealing', 'telling lies', 'adultery', and 'consuming intoxicants'.[60] Some verses are given here.

Rakhine Thu Mrat: Laukathara Pyo,
Part 1, Verse 15, my translation.
Please see the Diagram-3 for the Burmese.

Everyone has to learn;
There exists arts and science
and vast knowledge;
That man may learn to become learned.
It may be hard to master
every branch of arts and science.
But master a discipline of knowledge
So that you may bring wealth
to your family and society.
Just like the chicken night vision
If you are blind of knowledge
People will scorn and you will face hardship.
Have clear vision of future and don't lapse;
Don't let yourself laughed at in old age.

---

[60] Poor Senior General Saw Maung missed this part and he died of alcoholism! In reality, most Myanmar ignores this advice.

Diagram-3
Lauka thara pyo
verse 15 with my translation

ရခိုင်သူမြတ်   လောကသာရပျို့

၁၅။။ သူတော်တကာ၊ တတ်စရာသား၊

အင္ဂါရသ၊ သိပ္ပအပြား

အတတ်များကို ၊ မှတ်သားသတိ

ပညာရှိတို့၊ တတ်သိအပ်စွ။

ထိုသိပ္ပကို

နှံ့မျှလုံးခြို၊ မတတ်တုံလည်း

တာစံစံတစ်ခု၊ တတ်အောင်ပြုရ၍

လူမှုအိမ်ထောင် ှ စီးပွားဆောင်လော။

ညွှန့်မျှောင်မသိ-၊ ကြက်မျက်စိသို့

မိမိကိုယ်ဖို့၊ အတတ်ချို့သော်

သူတို့ပြစ်တင်၊ ဆင်းရဲဖျင်အံ့ ^{2}။

ထင်ထင်မျက်မြင်၊ မကောင်းရော်သည်

အိုသော် သူမရယ်စေနှင့်မင်း ^{5}။

Further, it urges to become a professional by learning a discipline of knowledge so that one can have a good living, Diagram-3. It teaches how to save money and accumulate wealth and look after the parents, relatives, mendicants, friends and servants with love and kindness. The teaching also highlights the need of practicing civility with due humbleness and politeness, and having a sweet tongue and controlling anger.

The twenty five verses (#23-47) of *Lauka-thara-pyo* Part-2, are meant for the kings and rulers, Diagram-4.

Diagram- 4
Lauka thara pyo
verse 23 with my translation

၂၃။ **ပြည်သူ ထွတ်ဦး**၊ ဘုန်းရောင်မြူးသည်
ရန်ရှူး လူဘောင်၊ ထွတ်ခေါင်**ရာစော်**
ဆုံးမနာလော့။

မဟာသမ္မတာ၊ **ခတ္တိယ**တို့
နေကျကျင့်ရိုး၊ ကောင်းကျိုးအလှူ
စွန့်ကြမူလျက်၊ စိတ်ဖြူပြောင့်စင်း
နူးညံ့ခြင်းနှင့်၊ သိတင်းစောင့်စည်း
မျက်နည်းသည်းခံ၊ **ဖြိုးဖြံ**သမူ
မပြုညဉ်း**ဆဲ**၊ ဆင်းရဲမရှာ
မေတ္တာပွားဖြန့်၊ လူ**အဂုန်**အား
မဆန့်ကျင်စေ၊ ဤသို့ရေသား
ဆယ်တွေ စောင့်ကြပ်၊ တရားကွပ်၍
လက်ယပ်ခေါ်ပြု၊ **သ္ကြိုဟ်**မူလည်း
လေးခုအစေ့၊ **ပြကတေ့ဖြင့်**
ကျင့်လေမကွင်း၊ ကျန်စေမင်း။

Rakhine Thu Mrat: Laukathara Pyo,
Part 2, Verse 23, my translation
Please see the Diagram-4 for the Burmese.

Oh King,
You are the head of the people
Brilliant with glory,
Leader of the society -
Listen to my advice!
These are the laws followed and practiced by
The First King Thamada of mankind
And all striving men of honor.
Charity with good virtue,
Self-sacrifice for benefit of others,
Service with honesty and sincerity,
Deal with humility and humbleness,
Observe Sabbath, control anger,
Practice tolerance, austerity,
Avoidance of torture,
Respect for the public opinion.
Uphold these ten laws of
King's precept
Treat everyone like your friends
With four friendship rules
Don't be negligent; don't make an exception.

It teaches to be a good king and ruler
abiding by the ten precepts that have been
prescribed and practiced since beginning with
the first King *Thamada* of mankind. The ten
precepts are the practices of (1) charity, (2)
self-sacrifice for benefit of others, (3) honesty
and sincerity, (4) humbleness, (5) Sabbath, (6)
controlling anger, (7) tolerance, (8) austerity,

(9) avoidance of torture, and (10) respect for the public opinion. The four friendship rules are (1) welcoming, (2) hospitality, (3) charity or generosity, and (4) looking after, especially during the illness and decent burial at death.

Rakhine Thu Mrat also asked the king to be expert in the art of war, not to neglect diplomacy and intelligence, to protect the territory and defend his people. He told the king that the country affairs are difficult to understand and hard to predict. Therefore, the king is advised to constantly consult with the ministers, intellectuals, and monks so that crisis can be prevented. More, *Lauka-thara-pyo* hands down the king seven rules of governance – (1) to love and cherish the Guardian Spirits of the country, (2) to respect the elders and relatives, (3) not to take women and children by force, (4) to manage the affairs with due consultation, (5) to forge unity, (6) to look after the intellectuals and monks who have come to him and invite those who are still afar, (7) to rule the country fair and lenient avoiding the extreme measures. The teaching highlights that if a king lives up the seven rules of governance his country will be pleasant and bright like a moonlit night free of clouds!

In the Part-3, verses #48-55, of *Lauka-thara-pyo,* the ethnic, duties and responsibilities of the *Ponna* are described and prescribed. To be brief Thu Mrat advised them to be studious, learned, dutiful, and responsible as per description and prescription given in the book. In Myanmar society *Ponna* is a Brahmin.

Diagram- 5
Lauka thara pyo
verse 48 with my translation

ရခိုင်သူမြတ် လောကသာရပျို့

၄၈။ ။ မှတ်ကုန်ကြလော့၊ ဗြဟ္မာ့နွယ်ရိုး၊ ပုဏ္ဏားမျိုးကို၊
ကောင်းကျိုးစကား၊ ငါလျှင်ကြားပိမ့်။ ရှေးဖျားကမ္ဘာ၊ အစစွာ
က၊ ဗြဟ္မာပိုင်းခြား၊ ဆေးသမားနှင့်၊ ဟူးရားကျမ်းမြင်[၁]၊
ကောင်းကင်နက္ခတ်၊ တတ်သည်တသီး၊ ယစ်မီးပူဇော်[၂]၊
ဖြော်ဖြော်မန်းရွတ်၊ ဂြိုဟ်နက္ခတ်သင်္ချေ ။ ဦးဆေးတခြား၊ ခေါင် ဖျား
ဗေဒင်၊ သိမြင်နှံ့စပ်၊ တိဝိကပ်နှင့်[၃]၊ ကလာပ်ဈုဋ္ဌိ၊ ဒဏ္ဍီဝိဒဂ်၊
ကျမ်းခက်ဗျာကရိဏ်း၊ တတ်နိုင်းတခြား၊ လေးပါးဤသို့၊
ပုဏ္ဏားတို့တွင်၊ မချို့ကျေးဇူး၊ အထူးသမိုက်၊ မျိုးလိုက်မှတ်
သား၊ ဆေးသမားလည်း၊ ဆေးဝါးတတ်ကျွမ်း[၄]၊ ဗိဇ္ဇောပြွမ်း၍၊
ဆေးကျမ်းထိုထို၊ ရသာကိုလည်း[၅]၊ ဖွင့်ဆိုတတ်ကျယ်၊ စိပ္ပါယ်
အနက်၊ လွန်လေ့ကျက်၍၊ ဓာတ်ပျက်သည်းခြေ၊ သွေးလေ
ချောက်ချား၊ သလိပ်ဖျားက[၆]၊ စသည့်ရောဂါ၊ အနာအမျိုး၊
ကိုးဆယ့်ခြောက်ပါး၊ အပြားပြားကို၊ မမှားလွတ်အောင်၊ ကုသ
ဆောင်၍[၇]။ အခေါင်သမားမြောက်စေမင်း။ ။

Rakhine Thu Mrat:
Laukathara Pyo, Part 3, Verse 48
Please see the Diagram-5 for the Burmese.

Record in your mind, Oh Ponna People, the descent of Brahmana! I will speak the words of benefit for you. Since ancient from the beginning of the world the Brahmana were of four disciplines - Medicine-man, Astrologer, Ceremonial Priest and Vedic Priest. With diligence, you must master your own discipline of science. Serve earnestly and make yourself outstanding. (This is a concise translation of the meaning of the verse omitting the poetic colors. SLM)

The terms Brahmin, Brahmana, Brahman and Brahma are very confusing. The term both Brahmin and Brahmana refer to a Priest of Hinduism or Brahmanism whereas Brahman is the creator of the universe and Brahma is the spirit, consciousness or essence of Brahman. In other words, Brahman is the Creator, Brahma is His Laws and Brahmana is His Order in the style of Buddha, Dhamma and Sangha. These definitions may be over simplification of the terms but it is easier to understand and remember. In India, the Brahmin (Brahmana) is one of the four castes; the other three are the Kshatriyas, the Vaishyas, and the Shudras.[61] It means it is hereditary; a person is born into it and dies in it. But in Myanmar it is a profession. When a person specializes and practices in the Vedic art, philosophy, science, and astrology and he is considered a *Ponna*. These days *Ponna* can still be found in the traditional wedding ceremonies, especially of the Rakhine people. The original Brahmin who came to Myanmar since the days of pre-Anawrahta are now all Myanmarese but the conch shell, Vedic arts

---

[61] Brahmana, Kshatriya, Vaisya and Sudra are mentioned in the Mahabharata. See http://www.harekrsna.com/sun/features/11-08/features1189.htm

and astrology are left knitted and woven in Myanmar culture. Colonel Sein Lwin, who became the President of the Socialist Republic of Union of Myanmar after General Ne Win in 1988, was a great Vedic researcher. He was the founding chairman of the Myanmar Vedic Research Society.[62] These days, many Buddhist monks practice the Vedic arts and astrology.

In a very similar system of Indian castes, the Myanmar also has four classes or 'amyo'. Literally, 'amyo' means 'kind or type'. For example Luaka-thara-pyo is a book of advice to 'amyo-laybah' or 'four kinds' of human, namely the *min-myo* (the royals), the *ponna-myo* (the Vedic professionals), the *Konthay-myo* (the merchants) and the *laythamar-myo* (the farmers). In modern days theses four kinds of human (amyo-laybah) evolve to four classes namely, (1) the ruling class (government institutions including the armed forces), (2) the intellectuals and professionals, (3) the business community, and (4) the farmers and workers. This was how U Nu's Pyidawtha[63] (Buddhist welfare state) plan as well as General Ne Win's Burmese Socialist Programme party[64] (BSPP) interpreted the traditional 'four kinds of human'.

---

[62] Burmese Buddhists do all important jobs as per Vedic astrology.

[63] U Nu's *pyidawtha* (Happy-Land) plan was introduced in 1952. I had a copy of English version until 1994. I lost it in one of many relocations. You can have some idea of it at http://buddhist-economics.info/papers/Heikkila-Horn.pdf.

[64] I am a graduate of the Burmese Way to Socialism Special Training Course, 1970, at the Central Institute of Political Science. It was a compulsory program that a scholar for higher studies at abroad had to pass.

During and immediate aftermath of the bloody 1988 uprising frank, open, and serious analytical discussion of the Myanmar political philosophy took place among the military elite, in contrast to Ne Win's 'Big-Father' phenomenon. They reached a consensus that a parliamentary form of military aristocracy, in the popular concept of Platos's 'philosopher-king' is the best solution for Myanmar.[65] The difference is that Plato viewed that philosopher must become king whereas the Myanmar military elite consented that soldiers must become philosopher and rule the country. It is a design in view of a system of the soldier-philosopher-ruler.

The 2008 Myanmar Constitution espouses the parliamentary form of military aristocracy in distinct characters.

1. The parliament must have the military representatives, which will serve as the 'guardian angels' of the State, Sovereignty, and Nation. The 2008 Myanmar Constitution Chapter IV, Section 74 prescribes the following provisions.

Chapter IV, Legislature, The Pyidaungsu Hluttaw, Formation of the Pyidaungsu Hluttaw

74. The Pyidaungsu Hluttaw comprises of the following two Hluttaws :
(a) in accord with the provisions of Section 109, the Pyithu Hluttaw formed with

---

[65] Information I gathered from my close friends in the Myanmar military circle.

Hluttaw representatives elected on the basis of township as well as population and Hluttaw representatives being the Defence Services Personnel nominated by the Commander-in-Chief of the Defence Services;
(b) in accord with the provisions of Section 141, the Amyotha Hluttaw formed with Hluttaw representatives elected in equal numbers from Regions and States and Hluttaw representatives being the Defence Services Personnel
nominated by the Commander-in-Chief of the Defence Services.

Pyithu Hluttaw
Formation of the Pyithu Hluttaw
109. The Pyithu Hluttaw shall be formed with a maximum of 440 Hluttaw representatives as follows :
(a) not more than 330 Pyithu Hluttaw representatives elected prescribing electorate in accord with law on the basis of township as well as population
or combining with an appropriate township which is contagious to the
newly-formed township if it is more than 330 townships;
(b) not more than 110 Pyithu Hluttaw representatives who are the Defence Services personnel nominated by the Commander-in-Chief of the Defence Services in accord with the law.

Similar provisions allowing 25% of the legislative seats in the Amyoyha Hluttaw (Upper House) and State and Region Hluttaws, and Self-Administered Zones and Divisions are also adopted.

2. The President and Vice-Presidents of the nation must have military experience. The Chapter III specifies necessary qualifications and prerequisite of the military experience is prescribed in the Section 59(d), whereas the Section 59(f) disqualifies Suu Kyi from the presidency.

Chapter III
The President and Vice-Presidents

57. The President and Vice-Presidents represent the Union.

58. The President of the Republic of the Union of Myanmar takes precedence over all other persons throughout the Republic of the Union of Myanmar.

59. Qualifications of the President and Vice-Presidents are as follows :

(a) shall be loyal to the Union and its citizens;

(b) shall be a citizen of Myanmar who was born of both parents who were born in the territory under the jurisdiction of the Union and being Myanmar Nationals;

(c) shall be an elected person who has attained at least the age of 45;

(d) shall be well acquainted with the affairs of the Union such as political, administrative, economic and military;

(e) shall be a person who has resided continuously in the Union for at least 20 years up to the time of his election as President;

Proviso: An official period of stay in a foreign country with the permission of the Union shall be counted as a residing period in the Union;

(f) shall he himself, one of the parents, the spouse, one of the legitimate children or their spouses not owe allegiance to a foreign power, not be subject of a foreign power or citizen of a foreign country. They shall not be persons entitled to enjoy the rights and privileges of a subject of a foreign government or citizen of a foreign country;

(g) shall possess prescribed qualifications of the President, in addition to qualifications prescribed to stand for election to the Hluttaw.

3. Buddhism is placed in a special position. It is specified in the Chapter VIII, Section 361 of the constitution. The constitution also recognizes Christianity, Islam, Hinduism, and Animism and pledged to 'assist and protect' them.

Chapter I
Basic Principles of the Union

34. Every citizen is equally entitled to freedom of conscience and the right to freely profess and practise religion subject to public order, morality or health and to the other provisions of this Constitution.

Chapter VIII
Citizen, Fundamental Rights and Duties of the Citizens

360. (a) The freedom of religious right given in Section 34 shall not include any economic, financial, political or other secular activities that may be associated with religious practice.

(b) The freedom of religious practice so guaranteed shall not debar the Union from enacting law for the purpose of public welfare and reform.

361. The Union recognizes special position of Buddhism as the faith professed by the great majority of the citizens of the Union.

362. The Union also recognizes Christianity, Islam, Hinduism and Animism as the religions existing in the Union at the day of the coming into operation of this Constitution.

363. The Union may assist and protect the religions it recognizes to its utmost.

The power structure prescribed in the 2008 Constitution is incredibly Myanmarese[66] –a continuation of time and space. One may not be able to step into the same river twice[67] but we cannot dispute the stream of continuity. In this way the social order flourishes as an integral part of the political system in Myanmar since the days of antiquity. The traditional royals and their soldier class (Thamada and Kshatriya) are made president, vice-presidents and parliamentarians. At the same time Buddhism is honored in its special position.

It is under this Myanmar Socio-Political Order that the Suu Kyi must be considered. As of August 06, 2014, she has collected 5 million signatures in her movement to become the president of Myanmar.[68] The signatures demand repealing of the 2008 Myanmar Constitution Section 59(f), which is one of the seven "Qualifications of the President and Vice-Presidents," and dictates "shall he himself, one of the parents, the spouse, one of the legitimate children or their spouses not owe allegiance to a foreign power, not be subject of a foreign power or citizen of a

---

[66] This term 'Myanmarese' here is the same as 'Burmese-ness' used in my book *Burma Nationalism and Ideology*, University Press Ltd., Dhaka, 1989 (original edition), p102.
[67] Popular words of Heraclitus of Ephesus (535- 475 BCE), http://en.wikiquote.org/wiki/Heraclitus; for his philosophy see http://www.iep.utm.edu/heraclit/
[68] Reported by many media. For example see http://www.foxnews.com/world/2014/08/06/nearly-5m-sign-up-to-support-change-myanmar-military-drafted-constitution/ and http://www.irrawaddy.org/burma/nld-says-5-million-sign-petition-change-constitution.html

foreign country. They shall not be persons entitled to enjoy the rights and privileges of a subject of a foreign government or citizen of a foreign country." The Section 59(f) disqualifies Suu Kyi's presidential candidature because her deceased husband Dr. Michael Aris was a Britisher and her two sons are the British citizens. The signatures also demand repealing of the Sections 109(b) and 141(b), which mandatory assigned 25% of the parliamentary seats to the military representatives. In short, the signatures demand the military withdrawal from politics.

Her signature campaign is democratic. Nevertheless, in the context of today's Myanmar it can be argued that a person of paramount stature like Suu Kyi does not have to be a president to change the country and that the democratization of the country would be easier and smoother in the presence of the military representatives in the parliaments of all levels. In the initial phase of Myanmar democratization, it is the best to keep the military under the public watchful eyes rather than isolating them in the barracks. The military presence in the parliament not only allows the public eyes on them but also creates a venue of friendship and understanding of the people and military representatives. This is a great advantage in Myanmar transition from military aristocracy to people politics. So far, the parliamentary military representatives are very cooperative and facilitating in passing the laws and modernization of the country.

Forcing them back to the isolation in the barracks could make Ne Win reincarnated.

There are more important issues like the Kachin War, Rohingya crisis, unemployment, industrialization and globalization, economic emancipation, food autarky, agriculture and climate change, crime and corruption, clean water availability, health, education, and quality of life etc. It would be more productive and beneficial for Myanmar if Suu Kyi were to focus her energy and intellect in such developmental areas.

Suu Kyi, like the Bama populace at large, believes that Myanmar Buddhist society, culture, and people are democratic since the days of King Anawrahta (r. 1044-1077 CE), but it is the military (*Tatmadaw)* that is evil and has gone astray.[69] In light of the Myanmar socio-political order discussed here it is clear that the entire Myanmar society and people must change and educate with modern scientific thoughts and concepts. We have witnessed that the blame was put squarely on Ne Win, Saw Maung, and Than Shwe, and now on the armed forces (Tatmadaw). I view that it is very unfair.

---

[69] In this subject the reader may consult my earlier books.
Shwe Lu Maung, *Burma Nationalism and Ideology*, University Press Ltd., Dhaka, 1989, and
Shwe Lu Maung, *The Price of Silence: Muslim-Buddhist War of Bangladesh and Myanmar – A Social Darwinist's Analysis*, DewDrop Arts & Technology, USA, 2005

For examples:

1. The civil war that resulted from the question of federation, equality, liberty and justice is not the fault or the crime of the Tatmadaw.[70] It was generated by the Bama supremacy (see the Chapter 8). As a matter of fact, the peace initiatives came from Ne Win in 1964 and from Saw Maung and Than Shwe in the 1990s, and from *Tatmadaw* in 2010.

2. The Burmese Way to Socialism cannot be blamed solely on Ne Win. Aung San was a communist, the first General Secretary of the Communist Party of Burma (see the Chapter 7). U Nu was a (Buddhist) socialist, Aung Gyi was a socialist, Kyaw Nyein was socialist, and Aung Shwe, Kyi Maung, and Tin Oo were all socialists. As a matter of fact, the entire Myanmar populace was anti-West and anti-capitalist until 1988. Even now, anti-West stance is clearly seen in the Rakhine State and 969 movement.

3. Racism, especially anti-Kala (anti-Indian, anti-Bengali) and anti-Tayut (anti-Chinese), which resulted in the Citizenship Act of Burma 1982, was not brought about by Ne Win or Tatmadaw, alone. The Myanmar people wanted to expel the Indians and Chinese from the land of Myanmar. Two main consultants in the formulation of the Citizenship Act of Burma 1982 are the Rakhine intellectuals.[71] Today, the

---

[70] The war crimes at the battlefields are different from the causation of the war.

[71] See Shwe Lu Maung, *The Rakhine State Violence*, Vol. 2: The Rohingya, Shahnawaz Khan Publication (USA), 2014, p 107, and Shwe Lu Maung, *The Price of Silence: Muslim-Buddhist War of Bangladesh*

two houses of parliament that include Suu Kyi, and the people at large honor and uphold the Citizenship Act of Burma 1982.

Myanmar people must share the responsibility of the failures as well as the guilt of the crimes. I have opposed and fought against the military colonial dictatorship since the 2nd of the March 1962, the day Ne Win and his colonels seized power.[72] It is my own experience that the Myanmar people at large are the prisoners of the past, filled with pride and prejudice. It will be more beneficial for the Myanmar if Suu Kyi were to generate more moral courage to dispel off pride and prejudice from the Myanmar society.

It is under such politics of pride and prejudice that Suu Kyi must be judged.

---

and Myanmar – A Social Darwinist's Analysis, DewDrop Arts & Technology, USA, 2005, p 232

[72] Please see my earlier books, mentioned at the Appendix-2.

6
Military Withdrawal

It is important to know the strategies and tactics of the Myanmar military withdrawal from the politics. I shall try to highlight the key points here.

The 1990 election was held to the non-existent People's Assembly of the 1974 Socialist Constitution, which has been shredded and thrown into the dustbin by the SLORC, on the 18th of September 1988. At the same time the SLORC (State Law and Order Restoration Council) gave out crafty statements. Some recorded facts are given below.[73] The emphasis in italics is mine.

June 1989
43rd SLORC Press Conference held on 9 June 1989

9 June 1989: "In response to a question from the News Agency of Burma correspondent, information committee members said that Saw Maung, Chairman of SLORC, had on numerous occasions touched on the matter of transfer of power.
...
We cannot transfer power as soon as the elections are held. The government would be

---

[73] http://www.ibiblio.org/obl/docs/Statements.htm

formed according to a constitution. If the state power is hurriedly transferred, it would lead to a shaky and weak government. This can be worked out by any person with intelligence. Stability can be achieved only by systematically forming a government based on a constitution."

"At present, we have two constitutions in our country, that is, the 1947 Constitution and the 1974 Constitution. Of the two, the 1947 Constitution was drawn up based on the 1935 Act - the Government of Burma Act 1935 - in accordance with the Aung San-Atlee Agreement.......The 1974 Constitution was promulgated after obtaining the wishes of the entire people on many occasions. The difference between the two laws has been pointed out. The elected representatives can choose one of the constitutions to form a government, and we will transfer power to the government formed by them. We are ready to transfer power to the government which emerges according to the constitution. If they do not like the two existing constitutions, they can draw up a new constitution. Neither the Defence Forces nor the SLORC will draw up a new constitution. *The elected representatives are to draw up the constitution. If the people approve that constitution, we will transfer power as soon as possible to the government which emerged according to that constitution.* There should be no worry about the transfer of power. We are ever-ready to transfer power. We are just stressing systematic transfer of power according to the law. We do not want to hold onto power for a long time."

Senior General Saw Maung, Chairman of the SLORC, on June 09, 1989, clearly said, "The elected representatives are to draw up the constitution. If the people approve that constitution, we will transfer power as soon as possible to the government which emerged according to that constitution". *It was a form of the constituent assembly that the junta SLORC was going for in the 1990 election.*

To my amazement more than two hundred political parties joined the folly. I was shocked just like a thunderbolt hit me when Aung San Suu Kyi and her party National League for Democracy (NLD) marched dancing merrily into the carnival of election without a serious question of what came next. The NLD won a landslide victory. The election madness led to crazy confrontation at the end of the election.

The world was excited with the landslide victory of NLD. It was perceived as a sign of democratic majority of Myanmar people. On the other hand, the 1990 election result was nothing different from those of 1952, 1956 and 1960, in term of the political and voting pattern.[74] In other words, the 1988 pro-

---

[74] See my book *Burma Nationalism and Ideology*, University Press Ltd., Dhaka, 1989, Chapters 3.8 (p 31) and 4.1.

democracy uprising changed nothing regardless of its face value. Plainly put, nothing changed in the essence of the political value.

Exhibit-11
Senior General Saw Maung contrasts
democracy from confrontation

Senior General Saw Maung,
Press Conference, July 05, 1989
Ministry of Information Publication

ပါးစပ်နဲ့ ဒီမိုကရေစီကို အော် ရံ နှင့် ဒီမိုကရေစီကြီး မေပါ နိုင်ဘူး၊ အာ ဖြစ်လို့ လည်းဆိုတော့ ဒီ မို က ရေ စီ ဖြော ပြီးမှ (confrontation)လုပ်နေလို့ အယ်ထိုလုပ် ကောင်းမထဲ

be observed and democracy cannot be built by words alone. My concept is like that. Because, it is no good making confrontation after saying 'democracy'. It's too dangerous.

At the end of the election, which was praised fair and free by the world, Senior General Saw Maung and his SLORC told the elected people's representatives to draft a constitution because there was no constitution to transfer power since the election-winners rejected both 1947 and 1974 constitutions. He said that once the new election was held with due constitutional values and he would transfer state power to the constitutionally elected government. He emphasized that he could not transfer power to a constitution-less government because it is his duty to maintain law and order. Saw Maung was simply repeating what he said on June 09, 1989.

The election-winners demanded immediate power-transfer no matter what and asked the Armed Forces to go back to the barracks. Senior General Saw Maung and his SLORC labeled it 'confrontation'. Earlier in June 1989 Saw Maung said 'confrontation' is dangerous.

Exhibit-12
The military government
for a new constitution
SLORC's 106th Press Conference
October 19, 1990

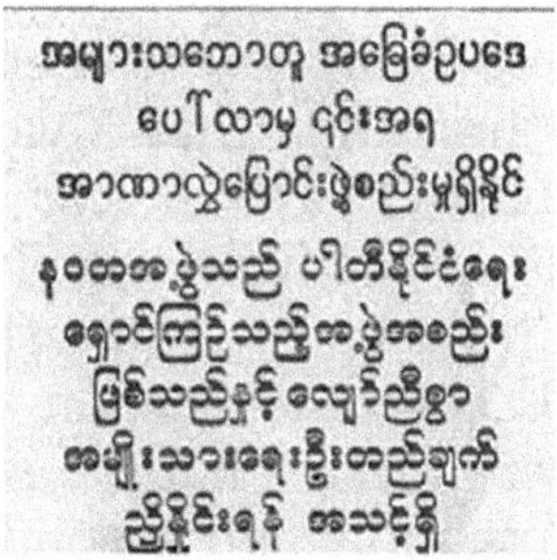

အများသ�‏ောဘာတု အခြေခံ‌ဥပဒေ
ပေါ်လာမှ ၎င်းအရ
အာဏာလွှဲပြောင်းဖွဲ့စည်းမှရှိနိုင်

နဝတအဖွဲ့သည် ပါတီနိုင်ငံရေး
ဆှောင်ကြဉ်သည့်အဖွဲ့အစည်း
မြစ်သည်နှင့် လျော်ညီစွာ
အမျိုးသားရေးဦးတည်ချက်
ညီနိုင်းရန် ဆသင့်ရှိ

Power will be transferred according
to the new contitution
SLORC is not a political entity.
Therefore, it will work for the
national cause.

The demand of the NLD for immediate transfer of power was roundly rejected and the junta remained firm in its stand that it would transfer power to a constitutionally elected government and as such, a constitution must be drafted first. The military government was ready to convene the Constituent Assembly to draft the constitution. The junta also conditioned that the political parties were not the sole owner of the constitution, which in fact was also a concern of the national races, farmers, workers, Armed Forces and civil service personnel. Then, the military government highlighted that Tatmadaw had neither political ambition nor political ideology but would strive for the emergence of a constitution in view of the national cause. These points were presented by the representatives of the military government at its 105th Press Conference at the Defence Ministry Guest Hall on October 05, 1990.[75] This was the first time that Myanmar Armed Forces (Tatmadaw) gave a clear indication of its intention of actively involving in the constitution draft in the interest of national cause. The NLD and the election-winners were greatly upset and flatly rejected the Constituent Assembly and a political place for the *Tatmadaw*.

Consequently, the tension arose and the political parties were 'disciplined' by making them 'illegal' and arresting many of the party leaders and workers. The world, in particular India, Europe and America, raged with anger, imposed sanctions, and awarded various 'Rights' and 'Courage' awards, including Nobel Peace Prize, to Aung San Suu Kyi. The world historical records showed that the military

---

[75] State Law and Order Restoration Council Press Conferences, Volume 7, published by the Ministry of Information, News & Magazine Enterprise, January 1990, pp 355-364.

junta broke the promise, did not transfer power and thus dishonored the election. This is what you will read in a media report or a history book on the account of the '1990 election and confrontation'. On the other hand, it should not be overlooked that the Saw Maung, chief of the military government, SLORC, clearly said it would be for a constituent assembly on June 9, 1989, and did offer them the Constituent Assembly, which would be extended with the representatives from the 135 national races, farmers, workers, Armed Forces, civil servants, intellectuals and professionals.

The confrontation got nasty. Suu Kyi was detained and the United States and European countries imposed the economic sanctions. The confrontation took a turn in 1995 when Senior General Than Shwe, who transformed the State Law and Order Restoration Council (SLORC) to the State Peace and Development Council (SPDC), convened the National Convention for constitution drafting. In 1992, Than Shwe succeeded Saw Maung when the latter retired due to health reason.[76] The election-winners were divided into factions; some joined the National Convention and some simply abandoned the party leadership with disappointment. The National Convention was

---

[76] Saw Maung's diabetes became complicated due his heavy drinking, probably out of stress. I was told by a person close to the ruling circle that he was deeply sad on account of the 1988 event, which he took sole responsibility. He died in 1997. My sources discard the news that he was removed by a quiet coup d'état staged by Than Shwe.

composed of the representatives from one hundred and thirty five national races, political parties, Armed Forces, Police Force, farmers, workers, intellectuals and professionals. Some of the armed guerrilla factions also made peace with the junta and joined the National Convention. The National Convention was the first step of the SPDC's 7-point road map[77] to democracy.

(1) Convening of the National Convention
(2) After the successful holding of the National Convention, step by step implementation of the process necessary for the emergence of a genuine and disciplined democratic system.
(3) Drafting of a new constitution in accordance with basic principles and detailed basic principles laid down by the National Convention.
(4) Adoption of the constitution through national referendum.
(5) Holding of free and fair elections for Pyithu Hluttaws (Legislative bodies) according to the new constitution.
(6) Convening of Hluttaws attended by Hluttaw members in accordance with the new constitution.
(7) Building a modern, developed and democratic nation by the state leaders

---

[77] "The New Light of Myanmar" (Internet version) 21 September 2003, downloaded from http://www.ibiblio.org/obl/docs/rallies-etc..htm on August 23, 2012.

elected by the Hluttaw; and the government and other central organs formed by the Hluttaw.

Suu Kyi opposed the National Convention and confronted the crafty junta. Many of Suu Kyi's disciples staged protests both at home and abroad. The most remarkable one was the protest dubbed 'saffron revolution' by the Buddhist monks in 2007. Many monks were de-robed, jailed or forced to escape the persecution and became displaced refugees. While I condemned the military suppression of the peaceful demonstration I was greatly concerned with the rise of the Buddhist clergy. I have seen Bangladesh rolling back to conservatism and theocracy with the rise of the Islamic clergy in Bangladesh in 1980s. The rise of the clergy in the political arena is always a concern wherever it may be.

During her twenty one years of confrontation from 1990 to 2011 Suu Kyi spent most of her time under house arrest with her female employees. While she was confined, the military government concluded its 7-step roadmap, a new constitutional government led by President U Thein Sein was sworn on March 30, 2011.

Exhibit-13
President Thein Sein and the Vice-Presidents sworn in.
March 30, 2011
(Kyaymon March 31, 2011)

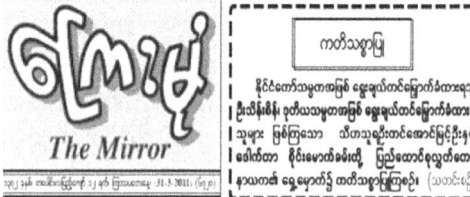

Suu Kyi's party NLD and its allies boycotted the 2010 election but joined the April 2012 by election when the Myanmar Election Commission relaxed the election rules that barred Suu Kyi running for the parliament. Suu Kyi was elected to lower house (Pyithu Hluttaw) from Kawhmu constituency and sworn in as a member parliament on May 02, 2012. Hereby the confrontation ended. She ended it just to accept a constitution that was suggested by the military junta in 1990—a constitution where there is a place for the Tatmadaw.

Exhibit-14
Suu Kyi and new MPs
sworn in the *Pyithu Hluttaw*
May 02, 2012.

Kyaymon May 03, 2012

The 2008 Constitution that she accepts now has given 25% of the parliamentary seats at all levels to the military representatives[78] and the president to be elected by the Presidential Electoral College[79] must be a person with military experience.[80] On these

---

[78] Myanmar Constitution 2008, Chapter 4, Section 74 , 109, 109(b), 141, and 141(b)

[79] Myanmar Constitution 2008, Chapter 3, Section 60.

[80] Myanmar Constitution 2008, Chapter 3, Section 59(d).

ground, it is reasonable to conclude that she wasted twenty two years from 1990 to 2012 with her counter productive confrontation policy. Myanmar could have gained the same value of democracy twenty years earlier.

Today, Suu Kyi demands for the repeal of the Constitution Section 59(f) that disqualifies her presidential candidature, and also to erase the Constitution Sections 109 and 141 that give the military 25% of the parliamentary seats. It obviously is the same old tactics of a Bama aristocrat, penny wise and dollar foolish. The military withdrawal from politics is different from the confinement of the military in the barracks. Suu Kyi's tactics are designed for the latter without being able to achieve the former.

The confrontation is Suu Kyi's political romanticism that lacks pragmatism and common sense. It is under such infantile political disorder that Suu Kyi must be judged.

7
A romantic Buddhist warrior?

"I would like to stay away from politics. But the present crisis is a national concern and I as my father's daughter should not escape from duty. This movement actually is the second struggle for independence." Aung San Suu Kyi, 26 August, 1988.

Exhibit-8
Aung San and
the Communist Party of Burma

COMMUNIST PARTY OF BURMA

Leaders

Thakin
Aung San

Thakin
Soe

Thakin
Thein Phay

Thakin
Than Tun

Thakin Zin

Thakin Ba
Thein Tin

This is a web clip from www.cpburma.org as of July 31, 2012. I have inserted the names of the leaders in English. (SLM)

Not only her entry to politics is romantic but also her name itself is equally romantic. Aung San Suu Kyi literally means the union of Aung San and Kyi. Aung San is her father and Khin Kyi is her mother. It is quite a romantic name reflecting the love affair of her parents. 'Suu' is unique to her. That is why she is commonly called Ma (Ms) Suu, Daw (Madam) Suu, Auntie Suu, Mama (Sister) Suu, Mrs. Suu Aris, and now Phawh-phawh (Grandma) Suu. In the classic Myanmar culture, calling her Daw Suu is respectful and friendly. The term Suu Kyi that I use here is more of a western culture.

Aung San is well known and his life history is the talk of the town. As I grew up I learned that he met Ms. Khin Kyi, a nurse by profession, when he was hospitalized from a sickness in 1942. She was a younger sister of Daw Khin Gyi who was married to Thakin Than Tun, Chairman of the Communist Party of Burma (BCP). As a matter of fact Aung San was the founding chairman of BCP. According to the http://www.cpburma.org/ the BCP was founded on August 15, 1939 and was headed by Aung San as its General Secretary in the fashion of the Communist Party of the Soviet Union.

Aung San left the party to lead the revolution against the British colonial rule and was among the legendary Thirty Comrades who established the Burma Independence Army (BIA), known as the *Bamâ Tatmadaw* in Burmese, with the help of the Imperial

Japanese Government in 1941. He was the Japanese-trained commander-in-chief with the rank of major general. Shoulder to shoulder with the Imperial Japanese Army the BIA drove the British Colonialist out of Burma in 1941, just to become a Japanese colony. In 1945, with anger over the Japanese's sham independence given to Myanmar, the BIA switched the alliance, became part of the Allied Forces led by the United States and helped the British reoccupied Burma. Aung San became president of the Anti-Fascist People's Freedom League (AFPFL) in Burma's continued struggle for independence. In 1947, he was elected to the Constituent Assembly and appointed as the prime minister. While he was negotiating the final bid of independence with the British government the assassins gunned him down along with his cabinet members on July 19, 1947. Daw Suu, born on June 19, 1945, was just two years old then. In light of this heroic legend and unfortunate end of her father she is loved and honored with due respect by Myanmar people.

In our student politics of 1960s Aung San was always there but his children never came into our discussion. I visited Aung San's house, a British Colonial architecture, at Natmauk Road, Rangoon, in 1963, and his parents' home, a traditional Myanmar design, in the City of Natmauk, Magway Division, Central Burma, in 1969. The City of Natnauk, once a major center of the Myanmar Imperial Order, was a run-down city under the Burmese

Way to Socialism in 1969. Except for the memories of Aung San his family was almost invisible to the Myanmar people at large.

It was in the stormy days of 1988 uprising that 'Daw Suu' came in like a thunderbolt striking everyone with awe and wonder. It was a surprise to the people. She was a heavyweight with the name 'Aung San' but a novice in politics and, as such, she was no match to the crafty soldier-politicians of Burma; nevertheless, the military junta would not be able to knock her out.

World News

Aung San Suu Kyi: Symbol of Burma's Free Soul

Shwe Lu Maung

In early 1989 while Aung San Suu Kyi was happily and boldly campaigning for her National League for Democracy (NLD), looking forward to the day of election on 27 May 1990, she confidently said, "I believe I must now call myself a politician." Thus,

In 1992, I wrote an article on her for the Illustrated Weekly news journal of Dhaka, Bangladesh. Since it reflects the early days of Daw Suu's political life, from a totally different angle from what the world sees, I here reproduce my 1992 article[81] that was published in the issue of Friday 15 May 1992, Illustrated Newsweekly, Dhaka, Bangladesh. The article gives her political situation in 1992 and lays foundation for further discussion. It reads as follow.

---

[81] Bangladesh officially uses British English. Therefore, the article is in British English.

In early 1989 while Aung San Suu Kyi was happily and boldly campaigning for her national League for Democracy (NLD), looking forward to the day of election on 27 May 1990, she confidently said, "I believe I must now call myself a politician." Thus, she entered politics following in the footsteps of her father, General Aung San. On 20 July 1990 her father's army which is now ruling the country under the name of the State Law and Order Restoration Council (SLORC) put her under house arrest.

However, the torch of freedom lighted by her shone brightly in the murky political scene. The NLD won 392 of the 485 seats (80%) in the election. She was awarded European Community's Sakharov Prize for 'freedom of Thoughts', Norwegian Rafto Prize for 'Human Rights' and, above all, the Nobel Peace Prize in 1991. Nevertheless, the NLD has not got power and she is not free yet.

As the daughter of Burma's national hero and martyr General Aung San, her entry into politics bears more emotional than political logic. In her speech delivered on 26 September 1988 at a public rally attended by half a million people, she said, "I would like to stay away from politics. But the present crisis is a national concern and I as my father's daughter should not escape from duty.

This movement actually is the second struggle for independence."

The political strength as well as the emotional weakness of Aung San Suu Kyi lies in the fact that her father was a much revered General— Aung San has been described as George Washington of Burma. When General Aung San was assassinated on 19 July 1947 by U Saw, a former Premier of British Burma (1940-41), with Brenguns stolen from British Army arsenals, Aung San Suu Kyi was just two years old.

Perhaps it was this trauma that kept Aung San's family away from politics. Her brother, Aung San Oo, the eldest of the three children, is now a US citizen and shows no interest in politics. Her elder brother, Aung San Linn, died (drowned in the Royal Lake at Rangoon) while he was just a child. Life took a new turn for her when her mother Daw Khin Kyi, a nurse by profession, was appointed the first woman Ambassador to India by U Nu in 1960. Aung San Suu Kyi had her early education in India. After graduating in 1964 from Lady Shri Ram College in New Delhi she went to study at St. Hugh's College of Oxford University and earned her bachelor's degree in philosophy in 1967.

After her marriage in 1972 to Michael Aris, who was an Oxford Don, Tibetologist and a family friend of her

British guardian Lord Paul Gore-Booth—a former British Ambassador to Burma—she became a research scholar at the Oxford University. No one thought that her happy family life as a mother of two sons (Myint San Aung, aged 19, and Htein Linn, aged 15) would come to an end abruptly in 1989.

She came to Burma in April 1988 to nurse her terminally ailing mother who died in December of that year. Unexpectedly she was caught in the mass uprising which was spontaneous but unorganized and leaderless. Former politicians and ex-military leaders approached her for providing leadership to the movement. In the backdrop of her apolitical life she made the decision to enter the political stage rather too quick. The mass uprising gained momentum and she delivered her first speech on 26 August, 1988. In their bid to face the challenge of students' unrest since March, General Ne Win, General San Yu and their successor Brigadier Sein Lwin (as per statistics of the General Strike Committee) killed some 7,000 demonstrators all over Burma. They had, however, been forced to retire in the fury of the movement. Dr. Maung Maung, a law expert and intellectual trained by Ne Win, was the President of Burma at that time.

The irresistible tide of the movement carried her into the centre of political arena. When political parties were allowed by the military government, (SLORC), which took over power on 18 September 1988 Aung San Suu Kyi became the General Secretary of the National League for Democracy. Until then she had insisted that she had no political ambitions, her participation was just a conscientious response as the daughter of General Aung San to the demand of the situation. She said that at a logical point she would quit politics. Before such a point was reached she was put under house arrest by the SLORC.

She has proved her high sense of patriotism. But questions arise: Was it right for her to accede to the persuasion of ex-politicians and ex-military commanders to become the central figure in the country's power politics? Would it have been better for her to remain neutral in the power game and play the role of a mediator between various factions of opposition and the military junta as she first proposed on 15 August 1988?

There is no question about her personal integrity or leadership quality. And beyond doubt she knows Burmese politics intellectually. Now she is learning Burmese political psychology, behaviour and tactics at a great cost. Her NLD which won the election on the strength of her image has disowned her. It is not wrong to say that ex-politicians and ex-military commanders exploited her patriotism and conscience thus making a scandalous sacrifice of high intellectual force in their dirty encounter with Ne Win, their sworn enemy.

Aung San Suu Kyi is not simply a prisoner of SLORC, but is a prisoner of her beloved country— Union of Myanmar. On 19 June this year she will be celebrating her 47th birthday all by herself. How many birthdays she has thus to celebrate alone is what naturally causes deep concern around the world." End of the article.

On June 19, 2012 she was free to celebrate her 67th birthday with friends and her party members. Twenty years have slipped away like a breeze never to return since Illustrated Weekly, Dhaka, Bangladesh, published my article in 1992. Nevertheless, I still ask the same question –

"Would it have been better for her to remain neutral in the power game and play the role of a mediator between various factions of opposition and the military junta as she first proposed on 15 August 1988?" I believe that if she had remained neutral in the power game in 1988 and mediated between the ruled and the ruler the bloodshed of the September 18th, 1988, could have been prevented. The transit from military aristocracy to democracy could have been faster as well as smoother.

Exhibit-9
The Rakhine State Riot

Myanmar forces deployed to quell **riots** - Aljazeera

www.aljazeera.com/news/asia-pacific/.../20126111011131776888.htm...

Jun 11, 2012 – Myanmar forces deployed to quell **riots** ... The **Rohingya** are a Muslim ethnic group from the northern **Rakhine** state of western Myanmar, ...

Violence Escalates in Burma's **Rakhine** State

www.voanews.com/content/violence...in...rakhine.../1205821.html

Jun 11, 2012 – The **riots** began after 10 ethnic-**Rohingya** Muslims were mobbed and murdered by ethnic **Rakhines**, in retaliation for the gang-rape of a ...

In the aftermath of the sectarian killing between the Rakhine Buddhists and Rohingya Muslims in June and July 2012, Myanmar seems to be slipping away into the dark chasm of racism in defiance to her strive for the democratic reforms. Once again, just like in 1988 and 1990, millions of people, including the Rohingya, look up at her for their freedom, democracy, human rights and justice. It is a big expectation resting on her shoulder. Will she meet the expectation or will she flunk?

Now, when it comes to the Rohingya the popular view is that they are illegal immigrants from East Pakistan, which became Bangladesh in 1971. The Myanmar people generously inflict discrimination and hatred upon the Rohingya with the view that they are the British colonial era immigrants. The sad and most undemocratic part is that the Rohingya are given *no* chance to defend their case before the law. On the other hand, there exists historical records as well as evidence from the modern molecular genetics indicating that the Rohingya probably are the most indigenous people[82] and many of them may well be the Muslim descendants of the Arakan Empire (Map-5), 1430 to 1784 CE.[83] The Arakan Empire weakened and was finally conquered and annexed by Myanmar King Bodaw in 1784. Hence, they are qualified to be a national race of Myanmar even under the most discriminatory law of the Citizenship Act 1982.[84]

In view of this historical reality the Rohingya people have been putting up their demand for the right to citizenship.

However, Daw Suu is in a position to mediate the dispute in her capacity of the Nobel Peace Laureate and leader of the opposition. Nonetheless, she declined to do so in fear of offending her party and constituency. Her party views that the Rohingya are the illegal Bengali immigrants. She cannot go against the will of her constituency, Kawhmu, that elected her into the Pyithu Hluttaw, the lower house of the Parliament. Just like most of the Burma Proper area, Kawhmu constituency is composed of almost cent per

---

[82] Shwe Lu Maung, *The Rakhine State Violence*, Vol. 2: The Rohingya, Shahnawaz Khan Publication (USA), 2014.

[83] The map of the Arakan Empire is based upon the chronicles given by Sir Arthur P. Phayre, History of Burma, London: Trübner & Co., 1883.

[84] For more information on the Rohingya please read my book, Shwe Lu Maung, *The Rakhine State Violence*, Vols. I & II, Shahnawaz Khan Publication (USA), 2014

cent Bama, Karen, and Mon national groups, Buddhists and Christians in religion. When she said, "The Buddhist should treat the Muslim minority with sympathy," at her meeting with the relatives of the Muslim victims at Yangon on June 7, 2012, she got into problem. Her people criticized that she was siding with the Bengali Muslim illegal immigrants. On the other hand the Rohingya Muslims expressed their feeling that sympathy could not be a substitute for their rights.

Map-5
The Arakan Empire, 1430-1784 CE

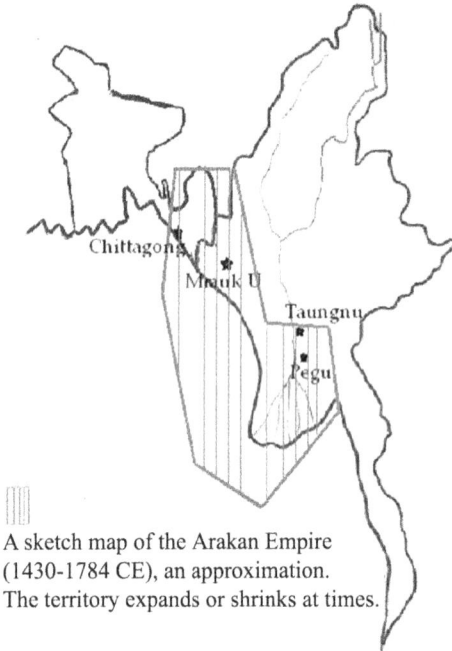

Chittagong

Mrauk U

Taungnu

Pegu

A sketch map of the Arakan Empire
(1430-1784 CE), an approximation.
The territory expands or shrinks at times.

In dilemma Daw Suu went silent. She did not even go to the riot infested Rakhine State, nor did she meet any victim or displaced person, regardless of Buddhist or Muslim. She did not see. She did not hear. She did not talk. Reportedly, she simply told the visiting Turkey Foreign Minister, Ahmet Davutoğlu,[85] that "she tries not to take sides, so neither of the groups will feel it is receiving unfair treatment".[86]

The irony is that neutrality, not taking sides, does not solve the problem. I view that in virtue of her Nobel Peace Prize she has to stand for the human rights above everything; particularly in this case, she has to rise above the nationalism or religion.

Exhibit-10
Nobel Peace Prize

The Nobel Peace Prize 1991
Aung San Suu Kyi

In the Nobel Prize 1991 Award Ceremony Presentation Speech, Francis Sejersted, Chairman of the Norwegian Nobel Committee presented the reasons why Daw Suu was awarded. Lest we forget the principles of the

---

[85] Ahmet Davutoğlu led turkey delegation in a fact-finding mission, visited the Rakhine State and donated items to the victims of both communities in August 8-10, 2012. http://www.aa.com.tr/en/world/72022--turkish-aid-reaches-out-to-arakan.
[86] http://www.hurriyetdailynews.com/fm-davutoglu-pledges-to-help-rohingya-muslims.aspx?PageID=238&NID=27556&NewsCatID=338

Nobel Peace Prize I have presented some excerpts from his address.[87]

Excerpt-1.

"Our fear and anxiety are mixed with a sense of confidence and hope. In the good fight for peace and reconciliation, we are dependent on persons who set examples, persons who can symbolise what we are seeking and mobilise the best in us. Aung San Suu Kyi is just such a person. She unites deep commitment and tenacity with a vision in which the end and the means form a single unit. Its most important elements are: democracy, respect for human rights, reconciliation between groups, non-violence, and personal and collective discipline."

Excerpt-2

"The central position given to human rights in her thinking appears to reflect a real sense of the need to protect human dignity. Man is not only entitled to live in a free society; he also has a right to respect."

Excerpt-3

"In recent decades, the Norwegian Nobel Committee has awarded a number of Prizes for Peace in recognition of work for

---

[87]

http://www.nobelprize.org/nobel_prizes/peace/laureates/1991/presentation-speech.html, accessed on August 17, 2012.

human rights. It has done so in the conviction that a fundamental prerequisite for peace is the recognition of the right of all people to life and to respect. Another motivation lies in the knowledge that in its most basic form, the concept of human rights is not just a Western idea, but common to all major cultures. Permit me in this connection to quote a paragraph of Aung San Suu Kyi's essay *In Quest of Democracy*:

Where there is no justice there can be no secure peace.

...That just laws which uphold human rights are the necessary foundations of peace and security would be denied only by closed minds which interpret peace as the silence of all opposition and security as the assurance of their own power. The Burmese associate peace and security with coolness and shade:

The shade of a tree is cool indeed
The shade of parents is cooler
The shade of teachers is cooler still
The shade of the ruler is yet more cool
But coolest of all is the shade of the Buddha's teachings.

Thus to provide the people with the protective coolness of peace and security, rulers must observe the teachings of the Buddha. Central to these teachings are the concepts of truth, righteousness and loving kindness. It is government based on these very qualities that the people of Burma are seeking in their struggle for democracy."[88]

Thus she was honored and praised in 1991. Today, the Rohingya crisis and the Kachin War challenge her more than ever. Tomorrow, the challenge will be stronger. She must boost her moral courage, show her fearlessness and stand up for 'human rights'. After all, she is the author of "Freedom From Fear." It is reasonable to believe that she is silent, not because of fear but because she is calculating her political gains in the Myanmar Buddhist society.

It is under this view of a Nobel Laureate romantic Buddhist warrior that the Suu Kyi must be judged.

---

[88] Quest for Democracy", in *Freedom*, pp. 167-179, esp. pp. 177-178, cited by Francis Sejersted in his speech quoted here.

8
Bama Supremacy

Emergence of Suu Kyi as the leader confirms the Bama (Burman) supremacy in Myanmar. The Bama supremacy was established by King Anawrahta in 1044 CE, Bogyoke Aung San revived it in 1947 and Aung San Suu Kyi validated it in 1988.

Suu Kyi is a leader born of chaos. It was the popular 1988 August 8 uprising that catapulted her into the supreme leadership in the merit of her birth. In the classification of Niccolo Machiavelli,[89] she is a *prince of fortune* or *hereditary prince*. In 1988, her résumé was simple and average: an Oxford socialite with a bachelor degree in philosophy, some research experience, no outstanding work experience, no career orientation up to the age 43, totally apolitical, away from Burma since 1960, never said a word against the military rule. The only strength of hers was (and still is) that her father was Bogyoke Aung San. The uprising that put her on the throne as the *hereditary prince* is popularly known as the Four Eight's - 8.8.88 or just 8888. The uprising forced the strongman General Ne Win to resign, ending his career of socialist military dictator. It also gave birth to a new generation of military leaders who were compelled to

---

[89] See Niccolo Machiavelli, *The Prince* (1513), translated by Daniel Donna, Bantam Books, 1966. You can read online in various web sites.

inherit General Ne Win's blunders, uphold the integrity of the armed forces, and obliged to put back Myanmar into her original 1948-path of democracy. In addition, the 8888 also produced a young generation of pro-democracy leaders, who were just in late teens in 1988. The military generals dubbed the uprising as the *riot*. The last socialist president of Myanmar, Dr. Maung Maung (1925-1994), a constitutional law specialist with double doctoral degrees, first from Utrecht University, Netherlands[90] and second from Yale, USA, recorded the event in his book *The 1988 Uprising in Burma.*[91] The original title was *The 1988 Riots in Burma*. The word 'riots' was changed to 'uprising' and the book was published posthumously.

The bloody event was reported in real time by the BBC, with Christopher Gunness in the field, and in 1989, a book on it was published by a distinguished journalist and author named Bertil Lintner under the title of *Outrage: Burma's struggle for Democracy.*[92] Popularly, it is called as the *pro-democracy uprising* by the mass media. However, Red Comrade U Oo Khin Maung,[93] called it *Paris Commune in Burma*; now I call it *Rangoon Commune*. He was then a Central Executive

---

[90] http://en.wikipedia.org/wiki/Maung_Maung
[91] Maung Maung, *The 1988 Uprising in Burma,* Yale Southeast Asia Studies (1999).
[92] Weatherhill; 2nd edition, 1995; the 1st edition was published in 1991.
[93] Red Comrade U Oo Khin Maung, a graduate of Rangoon University, who was given asylum by Australia in late 1990s, is a good friend of mine.

Committee (Politburo) member of Arakan Communist Party (ACP, now defunct) and Joint-Secretary of National United Front of Arakan (NUFA), which evolved into National United Party of Arakan, NUPA, in 1997. I recorded the concept of his *Paris Commune in Burma* in an earlier article[94] as follow.

During the peak of the uprising in late August, he came all the way from his hideout in the Bangladesh-Burma border, traveling more than 200 risky miles, to see me in Dhaka and discussed about the *Paris Commune in Burma*, to my disappointment.[95]

With his standard pleasant and humble smile, he asked me, "So, Ako Shwe Lu Maung, you believe that the military government will be overthrown this time?"

I answered, "I believe so, Ako Oo Khin Maung".

"How could you, when all what is going on is nothing but *a Paris Commune*?", he blasted me, still wearing that gentle and humble smile.

"How could you say that?"

This was all I knew to rebut at that time. I was taken absolutely unguarded. Today, time has proven that there was a solid substance in what he said. It deserves a closer

---

[94] The Arakanese Student and Youth Movements Series-4: The Third Dimension of 8.8.88.By Shwe Lu Maung *alias* Shahnawaz Khan, Arakanpost, Issue 5, July 2004,
http://shwelumaung.org/publications/series4.pdf
[95] Also see Shwe Lu Maung, *The Price of Silence: Muslim-Buddhist War of Bangladesh and Myanmar – A Social Darwinist's Analysis*, DewDrop Arts & Technology, USA, 2005. p 189

look, since it constitutes *the third dimension* of the 1988 democracy uprising. Today, I view that Daw Suu was a leader born out of *the 1988 Rangoon Commune*, which was more of an anarchic chaos than a pro-democracy movement.

A historical event that is known as the Paris Commune lasted 72 days from March 26 to May 30 in 1871. It is hailed as the first proletarian revolution by the leftists and scorned as the anarchism by the rightists. More than 100,000 men and women were killed or exiled when it was finally crushed. A critical analyst named Alexander Tracutenberg (1934) commented as follows:[96] *"The absence of a disciplined, well-knit revolutionary leadership both prior to and after the establishment of the Commune spelled disaster at the outset.* There was no unified and theoretically sound working class political party to put itself at the head of this elemental rising of the masses. Several groups competed for leadership--the Prudhonists, the Blanquists and the Internationalists were the most representative of them. And this doomed the Commune to continued confusion and indecision, to a lack of planning and of a long-range program. Piecemeal, day-to-day treatment of a rapidly developing revolutionary situation with utter

---

[96] See Lessons of the Paris Commune, International Publishers, International Pamphlets No. 12, sponsored by the John Reed Club, an organization of revolutionary writers and artists in New York. Third edition, 1934, at http://dwardmac.pitzer.edu/anarchist_archives/coldoffthepresses/tracutenberg/pariscommune.html, accessed on August 17, 2012.

neglect of tactics seemed to have been the practice of the leaders."

That was exactly what happened at 1988 Rangoon Commune[97] – 'no leaders, no plan, piecemeal, day-to-day treatment of a rapidly developing revolutionary situation, utter lack of tactics'. At the end, the Rangoon Commune was crushed by the Myanmar Armed Forces (Tatmadaw) on 18th September, 1988. The pro-democracy activists claimed that somewhere between 7,000 and 10,000 people were killed.[98] No leaders were visible during the crush-down. No illustrious leader came out to the street in those 40 days of chaos and turmoil. No leader stood in front of the helpless mass and said, "Kill me first before you kill these common citizens."

In spite of all these weakness I salute those brave people who died on the streets of Myanmar in 1988. Millions of people fearlessly marched in fifty seven cities across Myanmar. They called for democracy, human rights, open market economy and pluralism. When the leaders failed to realize their dream they embraced brave deaths on the streets and in the torture chambers. They were the forerunners of Tiananmen Square (1989) and the Arab Springs of the 21st century. Such was their courage and such was their dream that

---

[97] The readers who want to know more about the uprising are recommended to read the books by Dr. Maung Maung and Bertil Linter mentioned above.
[98] In the period from August 1988 to June 1992, I met more than 500 activists from various parts of Myanmar. Most of them asserted that more than 10,000 were killed. The international media is satisfied with a figure of 3,000. We may never know the truth.

the world never questioned what they meant by democracy.

Photo-3
8888 uprising in Sittwe
Photo Credit: Comrade Kyaw Khaing

The Photo-3 shows these courageous people from the Rakhine State. They braved the bullets and torture chambers for democracy, human rights, open market economy and pluralism. The poster in the lower right picture reads 'welcome to pure democracy'. Today, how sad it is to see that they are killing each other across the ethnic and religious lines in the name of nationalism and national security? And it is unimaginable that the world revered democracy icon went silent.

I was upset when my good friend Red Comrade Oo Khin Maung called it 'Paris Commune in Burma' in 1988. Nevertheless, by 1990 I accepted his view when more than two hundred political parties emerged to compete in the 1990 election held by the military rulers. I viewed the 1990 election a fake. I still cherish my view. There was no constitution and hence no parliament. The election was held in the design of the 1974 Socialist Constitution but the Constitution and its institutions, including the unicameral People's Assembly, were dissolved with immediate effect by the new military rulers known as the State Law and Order Restoration Council (SLORC) on the September 18, 1988, the day they seized state power.

The most significant landmark of the 8888 uprising is the confirmation of the Bama supremacy. From August 8 to September 18, 1988, it lasted 42 days only. In that short time it overthrew Ne Win and showed that the unarmed Bama people can undo the military might. The event ridiculed the ineffectiveness of the 40 years armed rebellion of the non-Bama peoples.

The big question is how Suu Kyi will use the Bama supremacy to establish a republic owned by the people, run by the people for the people in the line of Abraham Lincoln's "government of the people by the people for the people." At present the Republic of the Union of Myanmar is owned by the Bama, run by the Bama and it is for the Bama only. All non-Bama peoples are nothing but the auxiliary forces in support of the Bama operation and functionality. In other words, the non-Bama peoples constitute the slave labor in the society of Bama overlords.

The 2008 Myanmar constitution maintains the Bama supremacy in the same way as the 1947 constitution did. In my book *Burma Nationalism and Ideology*,[99] I described the 1947 Bama supremacy as follows.

"The parliament had two houses–the Pyithu Luttaw (People's Assembly) and the Lumyosu Luttaw (National Assembly). . . in the Pyithu Luttaw, 180 seats out of 250 belonged to Burma proper, whilst in the Lumyosu Luttaw, 85 seats out of 125 belong to Bhama (Bama)."

The picture of the Bama supremacy is clear. It is the Bama 180 votes versus 70 non-Bama votes in the Pyithu Hluttaw[100] and Bama

---

[99] Shwe Lu Maung, *Burma Nationalism and Ideology*, University Press Ltd., Dhaka, 1989, pp 27 and 34

[100] The official spelling is Hluttaw not Luttaw. I here follow the official spelling.

85 votes against non-Bama 40 votes in the Lumyosu Hluttaw. This democratic colonialism led to the non-Bama rebellion.

In the 2008 Myanmar constitution, the Section 109 'The Pyithu Hluttaw' and the Section 141 'The Amyotha Hluttaw' dictate the Bama supremacy. In the former there are total 440 representatives, including the 110 military representatives and in the latter total 224, including the 56 military representatives. The breakdown figures are given in the Tables 2 to 4.

The data presented in the Tables 2-4 clearly demonstrate the Bama supremacy in both Pyithu Hluttaw (Bama 317 vs 123 non-Bama, Table-3) and Amyothar Hluttaw (Bama 140 vs 84 non-Bama, Table-4), especially so because the military representatives are considered as the Bama representatives. General concept is that non-Bama revolutionary armed forces such as the Kachin Independence Army, Karen National Liberation Army, Shan State Army, United Wa State Army *et cetera* represent the non-Bama peoples, whom I call the Federating Nations.

Table -2. Myanmar Pyithu Hluttaw
Representation

Pyithu Hluttaw		
Region/State	No. of Constituencies	Count
1 Ayeyarwaddy Region	1-26	26
2 Bago Region	27-54	28
3 Chin State	55-63	9
4 Kachin	64-81	18
5 Kayah State	82-88	7
6 Kayin State	89-95	7
7 Magway Region	96-120	25
8 Mandalay Region	121-151; 326-330	36
9 Mon State	152-161	10
10 Rakhine State	162-178	17
11 Sagaing Region	179-215	37
12 Shan State	216-270	55
13 Tanintharyi Region	271-280	10
14 Yangon Region	281-325	45
	Total	330
Military Reps.	110	110
	Sum total	440

Table-3. Bama versus non-Bama representation in the Pyithu Hluttaw

Regions	No. of Constituencies		States
1 Ayeyarwaddy	26	9	Chin
2 Bago	28	18	Kachin
3 Magway	25	7	Kayah (Karenni)
4 Mandalay	36	7	Kayin (Karen)
5 Sagaing	37	10	Mon
6 Tanintharyi	10	17	Rakhine
7 Yangon	45	55	Shan
Bama total	207 vs	123	Non-Bama total
Military Reps.	110		
Sum total Bama	317 vs	123	Non-Bama total
Note. The military leadership represents the Bama people only.			

Table-4. Bama versus non-Bama representation in
the Amyothar Hluttaw

Regions		No. of Constituencies		States
1	Ayeyarwaddy	12	12	Chin
2	Bago	12	12	Kachin
3	Magway	12	12	Kayah (Karenni)
4	Mandalay	12	12	Kayin (Karen)
5	Sagaing	12	12	Mon
6	Tanintharyi	12	12	Rakhine
7	Yangon	12	12	Shan
	Bama total	84 vs	84	Non-Bama total
	Military Reps.	56		
	Sum total Bama	140 vs	84	Non-Bama total
	Note. The military leadership represents the Bama people only.			

In terms of the Bama supremacy the
2008 constitution does not differ from the
1947 Constitution. The 1974 Constitution does
not merit consideration because it was a
totalitarian Burman military colonialism. The
demand for a genuine federation, by the non-
Bama people will remain legitimate as long as
the Bama supremacy rules the country. The
genuine federation is defined as an equitable
federal republic, in which equality, liberty and
justice for all, transcending race, religion,

culture, and origin, will be incorporated with the philosophy of *we-the-people*.[101]

To be candid, as long as Suu Kyi does not speak out against the Bama supremacy it is legitimate to call her a racist.

---

[101] For more information on the genuine federation see Shwe Lu Maung, *The Rakhine State Violence*, Vol. 1: The Rakhaing Revolution, Shahnawaz Khan Publication (USA), 2014.

Epilogue

Perhaps racism is a variety of Freudian narcissism. According to the American Psychiatric Association it is known as the Narcissistic Personality Disorder (NPD) and characterized by the symptoms of being "excessively preoccupied with personal adequacy, power, prestige and vanity, mentally unable to see the destructive damage they are causing to themselves and to others in the process."[102]

When a nation has fallen into the realm of Freudian narcissism, and is "unable to see the destructive damage they are causing to themselves and to others in the process" it must be duly treated and cured. If a doctor is not treating the patient the doctor is guilty of malpractice. The same rule applies to the lawmakers.

Suu Kyi at present is a lawmaker and she wants to be the president of the Myanmar nation. We need to make sure that she is free of Freudian narcissism.

---

[102] http://en.wikipedia.org/wiki/Narcissistic_personality_disorder

Appendix-1
Min Hti Accountability

King Mun Hti (r.1279-1385 CE, Laung Krut Dynasty) was famous for his honesty, promise-keeping, accountability, and sincerity. This is the story the Rakhaing children learn from parents in their childhood, in my days. My parents taught us to be honest and accountable like Mun Hti, in every relevant occasion. I just hope this tradition still prevails. King Mun Hti's story goes as follow.

King Mun Hti cut off the first segment of his right pointer finger with his own dagger (Thanlayet) and with his own hand in compliance with his own law. The chronicles and oral traditions told us that tall and beautiful gold-gilded pillars of his Palace Hall became ugly and dirty with the patches of *hton* (a paste of calcium carbonate).[103] The *hton* is an ingredient of the chewing beetle leaf.[104] People picked up *hton* with the right pointer finger and apply it on to the betel leaf. They cleaned leftover *hton* by rubbing it against the golden palace pillars. In time, the palace golden pillars were filled with the patches of *hton*. One day, King Mun Hti hit maximum tolerance. He ordered everyone in the palace hall, including the ministers, to clean the golden pillars and the

---

[103] *Hton* or the calcium carbonate paste is made from the *mollusc* shells.

[104] For betel leaf and betel leaf chewing see http://en.wikipedia.org/wiki/Betel

hall. After, cleaning he issued the order that if any one dirty the golden pillars with *hton* again the first segment of his right pointer finger would be chopped off. One day the king himself pasted the *hton* on a golden pillar. A minister saw it and noted it with a witness. Upon his routine inspection of the palace hall King Mun Hti saw the *hton* patch and got furious. With anger, he asked the audience who did it. The minister replied that the king did it on so and so time at such and such date and produced his note and the witness before the king. King Mun Hti asked the minister, "Is it true?" The minister replied, "Yes, O' Great King." The king asked the audience, "Is there any body to dispute it?" Every one was silent in the palace hall. King Mun Hti, then solemnly declared, "In that case, I must cut off my finger segment." He pulled out his dagger (Thanlayet) and chopped off the first segment of his right pointer finger, right on his throne, in front of the full audience. Such was King Mun Hti accountability and sincerity. He punished himself for his crime that he committed against his own law. Even a Chinese scientist, Dr. Meng Yi, who became my colleague at the University of Missouri, Columbia, USA, knew about King Mun Hti story, though in a different setting. He, in 1998, told me that a Burmese was known in China for his honesty. His story goes like this. In the kingdom of that Burmese king every body was a thief, stealing goodies from his palace. He ordered that theft must be stopped and if any one stealing is caught the thief's hand would be cut off. One day the palace guards caught a thief red-handed and brought the thief to the king. To all excitement of aw and ah, it happened that the thief was the king's mother. The king ordered to cut off his mother's right wrist, with the proclamation "no one is above the law." I believe Dr. Meng Yi's Burmese king was King Mun Hti of Arakan.

Appendix-2

Books by Shwe Lu Maung

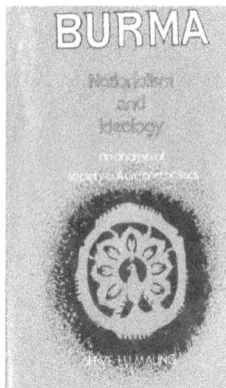

LC control no.:
89903911
Personal name:
Shwe Lu Maung.
Main title:
Burma, nationalism and ideology : an analysis of society, culture, and politics / Shwe Lu Maung.
Published/Created: Dhaka : University Press, 1989.
Description: xiii, 117 p. : maps ; 22 cm.

What happens in Burma has considerable implications for those who live in South and South East Asia. In this book a former Burmese guerrilla and a dissenter of the military regime, brings forth the complexity of Burma's present political and social dilemmas. He traces its roots in the historical and cultural diversities of Burmese people, in the feudal and colonial heritage of the country and in the stormy whirlwind of the modern political doctrines. It is the author's opinion that Burma today stands at the crossroads of socialism preached by Ne win, communism of the Burma Communist Party, democracy-based Federation of Burma and the disintegration of the present territory into feudal states. Shwe Lu Maung examines all the issues most succinctly and presents the readers with valuable information on Burma.

1999 re-publication:
- **Hardcover:** 117 pages
- **Publisher:** University Press Ltd. (July 25, 1999)

- **Language:** English
- **ISBN-10:** 9840511149
- **ISBN-13:** 978-9840511143
- **Product Dimensions:** 5.5 x 1 x 8.7 inches

****

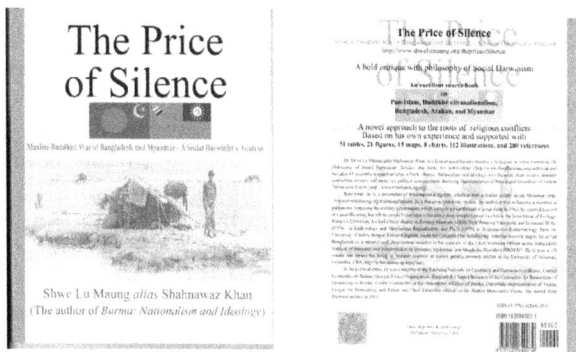

[US] Library of Congress
CALL NUMBER: DS528.8.B3 S48 2005

LC control no.: 2005906134
LCCN permalink: http://lccn.loc.gov/2005906134
Type of material: Book (Print, Microform, Electronic, etc.)
Personal name: Shwe Lu Maung.
Main title: The price of silence : Muslim-Buddhist war of Bangladesh and Myanmar : a social Darwinist's analysis / Shwe Lu Maung.
Published/Created: Columbia, Mo. : DewDrop Arts and Technology, c2005.
Description: 318 p.: ill., maps ; 27 cm.
ISBN: 9781928840039 (pbk.)
1928840035 (pbk.)

The objective of this book is to find ways and means to stop the on-going Muslim-Buddhist War of Bangladesh and Myanmar. In view of this objective, the book examines and gives detailed accounts of the causal factors that fuel the Muslim-Buddhist War. Three key contributing factors namely, 'Bangladesh Pan-Islam', 'Myanmar ultra-nationalism', and 'over-population' are thoroughly investigated.

The author tediously traced the historical events of Muslim-Buddhist War and rightly pointed out that today the war is simmering at Bangladesh-Myanmar border. The global warming and rising sea is gradually inundated the over-populated Bangladesh destroying the human habitat along the rivers and coastal area everyday. The agriculture and human habitat dwindles but the population grows rapidly approaching to the point of saturation at two hundred millions. At this point, Bangladesh will be swallowed by the chaos born of poverty, famine, and displaced people. Amidst the chaos and political instability, the Islamic Communes will emerge, in a similar style of the 1871 Paris Commune, to tackle the situation. It will be the time when the chaotic movement of the people out of Bangladesh will take place, destabilizing the region and flaring up the Muslim-Buddhist War of Bangladesh and Myanmar.

The author supports his presentation with 31 tables, 21 figures, 15 maps, 8 charts, 112 illustrations, and 280 references. The reader can listen to his videos at Amazon author page or at his website http://www.shwelumaung.org.

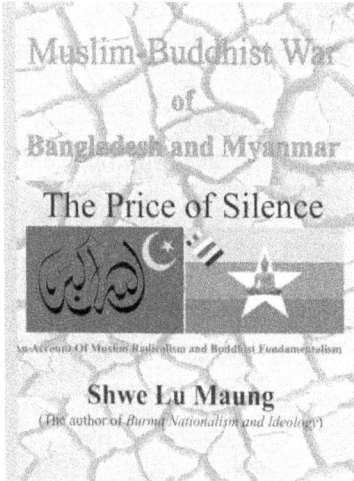

This ebook (ISBN 13: 978-1-928840-04-6) is the digital version (Kindle) of the physical book The Price of Silence: Muslim-Buddhist War of Bangladesh and Myanmar, 2005, ISBN-13: 978-1-928840-03-9, Library of Congress Control Number: 2005906134, Library of Congress Call Number: DS528.8.B3 S48 2005.

- **File Size:** 12520 KB

- **Print Length:** 455 pages

- **Publisher:** Shahnawaz Khan (May 31, 2011)

- **Sold by:** Amazon Digital Services, Inc.

- **Language:** English

- **ASIN:** B005GFJ3W0

- **Text-to-Speech:** Enabled ☑

****

The Rakhine State Violence
(in 2 volumes, total 622 pages)

Library of Congress Control Number: <u>2014902841</u>

Vol. 1: The Rakhaing Revolution
ISBN 13: 978-1928840-09-1
ISBN 10: 1-928840-09-4
341 pages

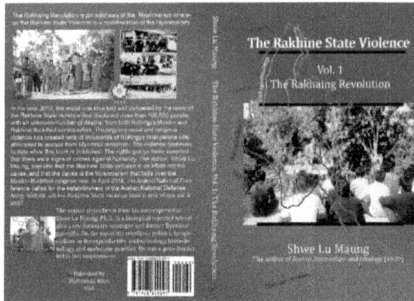

Vol. 2: The Rohingya
ISBN 13: 978-1928840-10-7
ISBN 10: 1-928840-10-8
281 pages

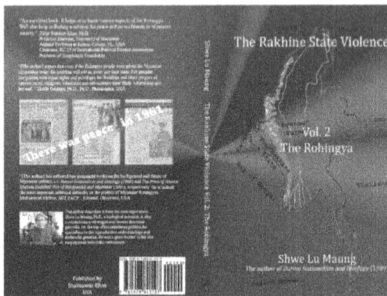

Description of the book

The Rakhaing Revolution is an antithesis of the Myanmarism whereas the Rakhine State Violence is a manifestation of the Myanmarism.

In the year 2012, the world was shocked and saddened by the news of the Rakhine State violence that displaced 140,000 people, with an unknown number of deaths, from both Rohingya Muslim and Rakhine Buddhist communities. The ongoing racial and religious violence has created tens of thousands of Rohingya boat people who attempted to escape from Myanmar terrorism. The violence continues to date while this book is published. The rights groups have asserted that there were signs of crimes against humanity. The author, Shwe Lu Maung, explains that the Rakhine State violence is an effect not the cause, and that the cause is the Myanmarism that boils over the Muslim-Buddhist religious war. In April 2014, the Arakan National Conference called for the establishment of the Arakan National Defense Army. **Where will the Rakhine State violence lead to and where will it end?**

The author describes it from his own experience. Shwe Lu Maung, Ph.D., a biological scientist by profession, was a strategist and theoretician in the revolution that aimed to decolonize Burma in order to establish an equitable republic in the philosophy of "we-the-people". On the top of his rebellious politics, he specializes in the reproductive endocrinology, biotechnology, and molecular genetics. He was a gene-hunter in his last employment.

Index

Burmese names are indexed in full name
Non-Burmese names are indexed with the last name.

Notes

www.ingramcontent.com/pod-product-compliance
Lightning Source LLC
Chambersburg PA
CBHW052106090426
42741CB00009B/1698